When a Marriage Ends

BY CHARLES L. ALLEN

God's Psychiatry
The Touch of the Master's Hand
All Things Are Possible Through Prayer
When You Lose a Loved One
When the Heart Is Hungry
The Twenty-third Psalm
The Ten Commandments
The Lord's Prayer
The Beatitudes
Twelve Ways to Solve Your Problems
Healing Words
The Life of Christ
Prayer Changes Things
The Sermon on the Mount
Life More Abundant
The Charles L. Allen Treasury (*with Charles L. Wallis*)
Roads to Radiant Living
Riches of Prayer
In Quest of God's Power
When You Graduate (*with Mouzon Biggs*)
The Miracle of Love
The Miracle of Hope
The Miracle of the Holy Spirit
Christmas in Our Hearts (*with Charles L. Wallis*)
Candle, Star and Christmas Tree (*with Charles L. Wallis*)
When Christmas Came to Bethlehem (*with Charles L. Wallis*)
Christmas (*with Charles L. Wallis*)
What I Have Lived By
You Are Never Alone
Perfect Peace
How to Increase Your Sunday-School Attendance (*with Mildred Parker*)
The Secret of Abundant Living
Victory in the Valleys of Life
Faith, Hope, and Love
Joyful Living
Inspiring Thoughts for Your Marriage
When a Marriage Ends

Charles L. Allen

When a Marriage Ends

Fleming H. Revell Company
Old Tappan, New Jersey

Scripture quotations in this volume are from the King James Version of the Bible.

Permission to quote from the following is gratefully acknowledged:

"See It Through" and "To-morrow" in *The Collected Verse of Edgar A. Guest,* © 1934, Contemporary Books, Inc., Chicago, Illinois.

Caring Enough to Forgive by David Augsburger, © 1981, Regal Books, Ventura, California.

Selected Plays of Eugene O'Neill, © 1946 by Eugene O'Neill, Random House, Inc.

"Have You Come to the Red Sea Place in Your Life?" by Annie Johnson Flint, Evangelical Publishers, a division of Scripture Press Publications, Ltd., Whitby, Ontario.

Library of Congress Cataloging in Publication Data

Allen, Charles Livingstone, 1913–
    When a marriage ends.

    1. Divorce—Religious aspects—Christianity.
    2. Christian life—Methodist authors, I. Title.
BT707.A45   1985   248.8´4   85-14168
ISBN 0-8007-1443-1

Contents

This is not a book on
how to prevent a divorce
——the divorce has happened——
let us go on from there. _____

When a
Marriage
Ends

One

Divorce

In 1890 in the United States, for every sixteen marriages performed, one resulted in divorce. By 1910 the figure had jumped to one divorce in every eleven marriages, and by 1920, it had further increased to one in every six marriages. In 1940 the ratio was one divorce in every five marriages, and by 1950 it was one in three. Today in America at least half as many people will become divorced as get married; in our large cities the totals are about equal—the numbers of those uniting in marriage and those breaking up are almost the same.

While divorce in many instances is a tragedy, in many others it is the best solution. More and more people are realizing that divorce is not always bad. In previous generations, many couples lived together whose marriages had died. The pressure of society helped prevent them from even considering divorce. Many times, a person who became divorced was almost ostracized. And many a wife had no choice but to endure an unhappy marriage; there was no such thing as community property laws and there was nothing they could do.

Today the situation is extremely different. Women have rights and privileges that were not dreamed of even one generation ago. The idea of "equal pay for equal work" was not even considered a few years ago. Today women are filling outstanding positions in all of the professions and in most every area of the economy. There are very few work areas in which women are not now participating. This has given women a freedom, an economic independence, and has changed their attitude toward marriage, making marriage something that they do not have to endure if they do not want to endure.

Also, America used to be a much more homogeneous society. People lived pretty much in the same community, had similar educational opportunities and common religious affiliations, and their family backgrounds were very much the same. They lived in simpler societies where they shared activities, liked the same thing, and had the same friends. Most of their time, other than when the husband was at work, was spent together.

In our urban society today things have changed vastly. So many married couples do not have things in common. Large cities provide a vast range of activities and contacts. Husbands have their business friends and their club friends, their golf and their athletic events, especially their own television programs. Wives have their clubs and social functions, and they too have television programs they prefer. Many wives work outside the home and are involved in a wide variety of activities. As a result, common goals and interests no longer hold the marriage together as they once did.

This is true of the family. There was a day in America when

most of the families lived in small towns. In the wintertime they had a fire in one room and all of the family sat together in that one room. They would talk with each other and would form really a family fellowship. Today it is different. Families live in centrally-heated and air-conditioned homes. Many nights, a man will sit and watch television in the den, the wife will sit in another room and watch her program and each one of the children will be in his or her room watching television, listening to the stereo, or engaged in whatever activity interests them. Today families are not nearly so unified as they were in past generations and in many instances marriages are not nearly as strong as they once were.

Why Do Couples Get Divorced?

Of course there are certain legal grounds men and women give for divorce, but usually the legal reasons are not the main reasons. Cruelty, desertion, neglect, adultery, drunkenness, non-support, insanity, conviction of a felony, and other grounds are named. However, the real reasons for divorce are as different as the reasons for happy marriage. The main cause of divorce is the disruption of the personal relationship between husband and wife resulting in conflict. Today temperamental differences, sexual dissatisfaction, and the lack of individual freedom are the main sources of conflict in marriage. Divorce is usually the result of tensions growing out of differences in the cultural backgrounds, patterns of living, personal habits, different value systems, and different ideals of a man and wife.

In counseling with many couples through the years I have heard, over and over, such expressions as, "He or she is not the man or the woman I married"; "I am just not interested in being with my wife or husband anymore"; "I want my freedom so I can live my own life"; "we are just not in love with each other any longer"; "he or she will not go to church with me"; "his or her parents have interfered with us too much"; and on and on. Today one of the reasons given for divorce is that one or the other will not have children. Even a generation ago that was not an issue; it was assumed that when couples married they would have children. But that has drastically changed. Many men do not want to be tied down to a family and many women have their own careers and do not want to be mothers.

Oftentimes jealousy develops between a husband and a wife as more and more they are competing together in the world. They may be following the same profession—medicine, law, or teaching—and one sees the other getting ahead. That is difficult to deal with.

Tensions Between Couples

When two people live together there are going to be tensions. There is tension between children in the home and certainly it arises between a man and his wife. That wonderful, exciting romance which led the couple down the aisle to that beautiful wedding just does not continue. Husbands do not spend all of their time courting their wives and being real romantic, and neither do wives continue to be that beautiful, glamorous, ideal, perfect person. So often, after the honeymoon the glamour begins to wear off.

Marriage is a glorious expectation, but also a serious risk. In former years marriage was based on the old authority-dependence relationship. The husband was the head of the house and made all the decisions, controlled all of the money, and was the authoritarian figure. That relationship has drastically changed, and as it changes we find that two people who are not dependent on each other oftentimes find it much easier to separate and to divorce.

Desertion

Records are kept of the number of divorces decreed in our courts but no record is kept of how many marriages are broken by desertion. Many times, it is the husband who leaves. But today, in numerous situations, it is the wife who leaves. Even though no legal action is taken to break the marriage bonds, still the marriage has ended.

Desertion can come about for many reasons—escape from financial responsibilities, escape from the burden of a large family, one or the other falls in love with some other person, and on and on.

As we study cases of desertion, we find that many times the person who deserts is someone who cannot face up to a particular crisis or difficult situation; he or she cannot bear the pressure. Their only way of handling it is to run away.

Illness in various forms is another cause of desertion. Alcoholism, drug abuse, mental disturbances, physical pain, and other illnesses can cause one to "walk away."

Desertion does not usually happen on the spur of the moment. It is the culmination of a series of conflicts and events. Often desertion comes as the result of a gradual dying of the marriage and of the home. Inability to personally adjust to some situation, be it sexual, cultural, financial, or temperamental, leads to conflicts that make the marriage impossible to continue and the marriage is broken, either by divorce in the court or divorce by desertion.

Many couples who are legally married have not lived together for years. In fact, many couples who live in the same house and are legally married still have not lived together in many years. Society looks upon them as married but their marriage came to an end long ago.

Involuntary Separations

Death, divorce, and desertion are the main ways marriages are broken. However, numerous separations, both temporary and permanent, come along in the life of a married couple.

One of the chief reasons for separation is that one of the marriage partners is transferred to another city by his or her company. The family is settled in the community and the man is told that his job is now in another city. It often happens that a wife says, "You can go but I want to stay here and maintain our home here. Our children have their friends here, they're in school here, I have my friends here and my activities. I do not want to move." When both a wife and a husband have good jobs and one is transferred, the other does not want to make the sacrifice of giving up that job, and thereby the marriage becomes a separation.

Marriage requires adjustments of two people. But often one or both of those two people are not emotionally or intellectually ready to make those adjustments. The circumstances of life are such that those adjustments cannot be made. It may be that the marriage was a mistake in the first place. It began wonderfully, but under the strain and stress it simply died. Differences in background, ideals, religious preference, handling of finances, emotions, relations with one's family, and many other things were such that one or both of the partners are not able to cope and the marriage is broken. Whatever the reason, we are living today in a society in which divorce has become a very important element.

This is not a book about how to prevent divorce. That is another book. This book recognizes that divorce has happened—now let us go on from there. In previous societies divorce was permitted only for the reason of adultery and a divorced person was considered to be disgraced. Today divorce happens for many reasons, and divorce can hurt in many ways; but divorce is no longer a dirty word.

Two

My Confidence Is Gone _____

Divorce is one of those experiences that can cause one to say and feel, "My confidence is gone." It is a very shaking and traumatic experience.

We would all likely be surprised if we knew how many people have suffered from lack of self-confidence. When I lived in Atlanta, Georgia, I was a member of the Eastlake Country Club. The great golfer, Bobby Jones, was also a member of that club and I frequently saw him in the clubhouse and on the golf course. Bobby Jones has always been a hero to me. I remember listening on the radio with bated breath as the sportscaster described his matches the year he won the British Open and the British Amateur, and the United States Open and the United States Amateur. I used to watch him play golf with great admiration, so one can imagine my surprise when once I heard him say: "Toward the end of the British Open one year, I lost my nerve completely. I stood there on the eighteenth tee with my knees knocking together. I can remember hoping my knees would stop long enough to let me take a swing at the ball."

Speaking of radio, I had a friend some years ago who was an outstanding radio commentator. He had a tremendous audience and people listened to him eagerly. But suddenly he gave up his career. One day I was talking with him and asked what happened. He said to me that he got "mike-fright" and could not overcome it. Every time he sat down before that microphone he said his voice would crack and he would begin to shake; so he had quit.

One of the greatest singers, if not the greatest of all time, was the wonderful Caruso. One night he delayed the opening curtain at the Metropolitan Opera for nearly an hour. What had happened? He simply got stage fright. He kept telling the director he just could not sing. Finally he got up enough courage to go out on the stage and start, and as he began to sing his lost confidence returned.

Sometimes our confidence is shaken by fatigue or by illness, but more often by some inner mental or emotional disturbance. There is the story of an earthquake that shook a small village. The people of the community were very much alarmed but they were surprised at the calmness and apparent joy of an elderly lady whom they all knew. At length, one of them asked the lady, "Mother, are you not afraid?"

"No," she said, "I rejoice to know that I have a God that can shake the world."

However, when one's own world is shaken it is not easy to rejoice. One of the reasons for a lack of self-confidence is the fear that we will not have the physical strength necessary to see us through. We need to remember that within every person there are certain physical reserves. A runner knows what it is to catch his "second wind."

Another result of a traumatic experience is that we begin to doubt our abilities. The truth is that no person has all of the wisdom and all of the ability, but everyone has some assets that can be used. The peacock has an incomparable display of colors, but it has a very wretched voice. The nightingale has very dull feathers, but it can sing in a glorious, soul-stirring way. The albatross can hardly walk, yet it can fly for miles over open water. If the peacock just listened to himself sing, or the nightingale just looked at its feathers, or if the albatross only tried to walk, each would be miserably defeated. Instead, each finds what it can do and does it.

In the midst of our depression, we need to pick out something we can do, and with all our might, do it.

Another thing that happens when we are depressed and feel hurt and defeated is that we feel we are "at the end of our rope." We need to remind ourselves to keep trying and life will open a new opportunity.

In 1809, Louis Braille was born in a tiny French village. His father was a harness maker. One day Louis was playing in the shop and stuck an awl into his eye. Infection developed and spread to the other eye and soon he was totally blind, never again to see the glimmer of light through his eyes.

His parents carried him to Paris and enrolled him in a school for the blind. The methods in those years were clumsy, learning was hard, and it was a discouraging experience.

One day an idea flashed into Louis Braille's mind—why not use dots as symbols for letters? Braille set to work and perfected a system and when he reached twenty years of age, his alphabet for the blind came into general use. It has remained in use to this very day.

A hundred years later the people of France honored his memory with a great celebration. In his hometown they unveiled a statue of Louis Braille, and at the unveiling of the statue, a dramatic thing happened. Scores of blind people standing at the base of that statue, when the cloth was drawn aside from the stone face, pressed forward with upraised hands. Slowly they moved their fingers across the face. They fervently thanked God for Louis Braille.

Braille might have spent his life in bitterness and in defeat. So likewise might any person who has had a defeating experience. But out of defeat can come our greatest victories. There is always another chance.

We have all loved the poems of Edgar A. Guest. Some of them are well known, but I am reminded of one that is not so well known. It is especially fitting for the person in the midst of a period of depression.

See It Through

When you are up against a trouble,
Meet it squarely, face to face;
Lift your chin and set your shoulder,
Plant your feet and take a brace.
When it's vain to try and dodge it,
Do the best you can do;
You may fail, but you may conquer,
See it through!

Black may be the clouds about you
And your future may seem grim,
But don't let your nerve desert you;
Keep yourself in fighting trim.
If the worst is bound to happen,
In spite of all that you can do;
Running from it will not save you,
See it through!

Even hope may seem but futile,
When with troubles you're beset,
But remember you are facing,
Just what other ones have met.
You may fail, but fail still fighting;
Don't give up, what e'er you do;
Eyes front, head high to the finish
See it through!

There is a wonderful little story that inspires all of us. After reading a sign in a store window, "BOY WANTED," a long line of applicants gathered at the door. One especially anxious fellow scribbled a note which he handed quietly to the interviewer: "Don't do anything till you've seen me. I'm the last in the line, but I've sure got the goods."

Three

The Feeling of Guilt

No matter what the cause of the divorce, many people believe there is something shameful about the failure of their marriage. Therefore, guilt is one of the issues that must be faced and dealt with.

To begin with, the parties involved seek to justify themselves and say it was not their fault; each lays the blame on the other person. Eugene O'Neill, in his play *The Iceman Cometh* (Act 4) captures this notion when he has one character say: "Can you picture all I made her suffer, and all the guilt she made me feel, and how I hated myself? ... I hated myself more and more, thinking of all the wrong I had done to the sweetest woman in the world, who loved me so much. ... I even caught myself hating her for making me hate myself so much. There's a limit to the guilt you can feel and the forgiveness and the pity you can take! You have to begin blaming someone else."

It is very rare when any divorce is one-sided; in virtually every case the blame and the guilt are on both sides. As a means of escape one seeks to fix the blame on the other. But eventually there comes that time when we begin to look inward and we feel guilty for our own part. Guilt can be one of the heaviest burdens one must bear. Guilt can make one physically sick, and it leads to depression, despair, and remorse. Guilt can make a coward out of you and leave you weak and filled with fear. Guilt can have a paralyzing influence and cause you to shrink back from life. This frequently happens after a divorce. There is a period when one just gives up and quits.

Somewhere I read a story about a boy in college who was sleeping very late one morning. His mother phoned and said to him, "Don't you feel guilty lying there in bed so late in the morning?"

The boy answered, "Yes, Mother, I do feel guilty, but I had rather feel guilty than get up."

And there are a lot of divorced people who feel guilty, rather than get up.

When I lead a tour group in Israel one of the things we do is take a boat across the Sea of Galilee in Capernaum. When we get there we can easily understand why this was a favorite place of Jesus to visit. While I'm there I always think of that experience when He was resting in a friend's house. The news spread that He was there and such a crowd gathered that they overflowed into the yard, completely surrounding the house. Four men came bringing a bed on which lay a man who was stricken with a form of paralysis. Not being able to get through the door of the house to Jesus because of the crowd, they went up on the roof of the house, cut through the roof and let the man down into the room where Jesus was.

Jesus saw the man's paralyzed legs, but He also saw deeper into the mind and soul of the man. He did not say, "Thy paralysis be healed." Instead, He said, "Thy sins be forgiven thee." Then Jesus told the man, "Arise, and take up thy bed, and walk." The people were amazed at what happened (Mark 2:1-12).

The trouble with the man was not paralysis. His physical sickness was a result of an inner sense of guilt and fear.

Fear can be a very paralyzing experience. Recently a mother was telling me of seeing her child run out into the street in front of an oncoming car. She said that she wanted to rush out for the child but suddenly she felt paralyzed in her tracks. She could not even cry out to the child. The car stopped, the child was safe, and immediately her paralysis vanished.

No doubt this paralyzed man in the presence of Jesus had a similar experience. Instead of an onrushing car toward his child, he saw the terrible judgment of God bearing down upon him. He had committed some wrong. His sense of guilt had destroyed his courage and the resulting fear had left him paralyzed.

What causes a feeling of guilt?

One might say that one feels guilty because he or she has done wrong. That is part of the answer, but not the entire answer. Guilt is caused by the wrong we do, but a lot of people do wrong without feeling guilty. Many people are not conscious of any mistakes or wrongs or sins in any way. Therefore, they feel no need of repentance, confession, restitution, apology or forgiveness. In some people, conscience has never been developed and in some, conscience has been killed.

Thus, there is a normal sense of guilt that is good. Guilt can be a sign that we still have a conscience and an inner spiritual life.

In his poem, "Song of Myself," Walt Whitman said:

I think I could turn and live with animals,
  they are so placid and self contained . . .
They do not lie awake in the dark and weep for their sins. . . .

While animals do not weep for their sins, it is also true that neither do they write poetry.

Another reason we feel guilty is because in normal people there are two natures—the good and the evil. We can agree with the great writer Goethe when he said, "It is regrettable that nature has made only one man out of him when there is material aplenty in him for both a rogue and a gentleman."

Both the rogue and the gentleman dwell within every person and each is struggling for supremacy. Speaking of one of his characters, H. G. Wells said, "He was not so much a human being as a civil war." I like this poem, though I do not know the author nor the source. Through the years I have used it many times:

> *In my earthly temple there's a crowd.*
> *There is one of us that's humble, one that's proud.*
> *There's one who's brokenhearted for his sins.*
> *There's one who unrepentant sits and grins.*
> *There's one who loves his neighbor as himself.*
> *And one who cares for naught but fame and pelf.*
> *From such perplexing care I would be free,*
> *If I could once determine which is me.*

At the age of forty-five Abraham Lincoln was a disappointed failure. In Robert Sherwood's play, Lincoln says, "You talk about civil war . . . there seems to be one going on inside me all the time. . . . It says in the Bible that a house divided against itself cannot stand, so I reckon there's not much hope. One of these days I'll just split asunder, and part company with myself."

But Abraham Lincoln did not "split asunder." Instead he found something to give himself to completely and in so doing he became organized and unified.

A guilty conscience never feels secure.

—Publius Syrus

Guilty consciences always make people cowards.

—Piltay

Someone has defined sophistication as too "smart" to feel guilty about anything you do.

Once a man was arrested and brought before a judge for a crime he had committed. "How do you plead?" said the judge. The man said, "I plead guilty and waive a hearing."

"What do you mean, 'waive a hearing' "? asked the commissioner.

"I mean," the man replied, "I do not want to hear any more about it."

Many times as we concentrate on our past mistakes they just get worse and worse. There comes a time when we need to get some new thoughts, some new inspiration.

I love the story of the social worker who kept trying to get a family to clean up their filthy, unhealthy home, but with no success. Finally the social worker hit on a new idea. He brought to the people the loveliest, purest, most spotless potted lily he could buy and put it on the living room table.

The lily sat in judgment upon that dirty, unhealthy room. Little by little the people there felt it and they began to make the room a fitter place for their new possession. Then the living room sat in judgment upon the rest of the house, so they cleaned that up too. And so it is as we begin to think higher and nobler thoughts. We gain inspiration to do what we need to do about yesterday's mistakes.

This is exactly what the Christian faith does for a human being. As we center our minds and thoughts on the "Lily of the Valley" we feel new inspiration and new courage and new joy. There is forgiveness from God and, receiving that, we can forgive ourselves.

Reflections on Forgiveness

In his book, *Caring Enough to Forgive,* David Augsburger offers these stimulating thoughts:

Where Forgiveness Starts
• Any movement toward forgiving begins with recognizing that we are in this pain together.
• Forgiveness begins as I see you again with love.

• The past exists only in memory, consequences, effects. It has power over me only as I continue to give it my power. I can let go, release it, move freely. I am not my past. The future is not yet. I can fear it, flee it, face it, embrace it, and be free to live now.

• Forgiveness is renewed repentance. The real enduring issues of justice, integrity, and the righteousness of right relationships are resolved and restructured into the restored relationships. So we are free to love, live, and risk again.

What It Isn't

• When "forgiveness" puts you one-up, on top, in a superior place, as the benefactor, the generous one, the giver of freedom and dignity—don't trust it, don't give it, don't accept it. It's not forgiveness; it's sweet saintly revenge.

• When "forgiveness" is one way, calling one person to accept the difference, absorb the pain, adjust to injustice—don't rush to it, don't close the case with it. It's not forgiveness; it's loving submission.

• When "forgiveness" distorts feelings by denying that there was hurt, disconnecting from feelings of pain, squelching the emotions that rise, pretending that all is forgiven, forgotten, forgone—don't trust it. It's a mechanical trick.

• When "forgiveness" denies that there is anger, acts as if it never happened, smiles as though it never hurt, fakes as though it's all forgotten—don't offer it. Don't trust it. Don't depend on it. It's not forgiveness; it's a magical fantasy.

• When "forgiveness" ends open relationships, leaves people cautious, twice shy, safely concealed, afraid to risk free, open, spontaneous living—don't forgive. It's not forgiveness; it's private alienation; it's individual estrangement.

It Never Ends

In a world of flawed communication, community is possible through understanding others. In a world of painful alienation, community is created by accepting others. In a world of broken trust, community is sustained by forgiveness.

Although in "forgiving," release unfortunately may be easier to achieve than reconciliation—

Although the one in error may choose to move over, away from, against the other—

Although one in weakness may attempt to live off of, without, in spite of the other—

Yet we dare not hesitate to take any step toward forgiving, no matter how faltering or fallible.

Yet we must not refuse to move toward another in seeking mutual repentance and renewed trust.

Yet we cannot despair of forgiveness and lose hope that reconciliation is possible.

So let us forgive as gently and genuinely as is possible in any situation of conflict between us.

So let us forgive as fully and as completely as we are able in the circumstances of our misunderstandings.

So let us reach out for reconciliation as openly and authentically as possible for the levels of maturity we have each achieved.

So let us forgive freely, fully, at times even foolishly, but with all the integrity that is within us.

When divorce happens one usually has the feeling of being wronged. Even though the individual readily admits that part of the fault is his, it is easy to begin to blame the other person.

When we feel wronged, we need to settle it. It is easy to put the burden on the other person and say such things as, "If he or she would admit his or her wrongs and ask my forgiveness, then I could forgive." In that sort of reasoning, we lift the burden

from ourselves and may go on feeling hurt and resentment and
even hatred without blaming ourselves.

Here I am not suggesting the restoration of the marriage; I
am talking about the restoration of one's own mind and heart.
Carrying the burden of hatred and resentment is more than one
should try to bear.

Once Simon Peter came to Jesus and asked the question,
"Lord, how oft shall my brother sin against me, and I forgive
him? till seven times?"

Simon Peter had gone a long way—further than a lot of people go. Seven times is a lot of times. I know some people who
have not been able to forgive one time.

However, Jesus replied, "I say not unto thee, until seven
times: but, until seventy times seven" (Matthew 18:21,22).

My Bible commentaries say that seventy times seven means
indefinitely. I am inclined to disagree. Seventy times seven is
four hundred and ninety times. I feel one might take that literally
and I suggest that when we have forgiven somebody four hundred and ninety times we might have done as much as we can.
After divorce it is easy to look back and remember wrongs which
the other person has done to us. However, now is the time to get
those things settled and settled forever.

One of the most difficult things to forgive is not some specific
act. No, it is the feeling that you did not get the attention or consideration you deserved. Recently I talked to a man who holds
great bitterness in his heart because when he was in college he
was denied a bid to a college fraternity. He felt slighted and rejected and through all these years he has held that resentment.

The hardest person to forgive is the one whom you have
wronged. Ask yourself a question. Who do you love most—the
person who does the most for you, or the person for whom you
do the most?

If you were walking down the street, which person would you
rather meet—the person who has done you a favor or the person
for whom you have done a favor? Does a mother love her child
the most or does a child love her mother the most?

Usually it is the one whom we have done something for that

we appreciate most. Likewise, it is far easier to forgive someone who has wronged you than someone you have wronged.

Remember—forgiveness of others is the price God charges for His forgiveness of us.

After Jesus had given the Lord's Prayer and had said, "Amen," then He felt it necessary to comment on one—just one—of the petitions in that prayer. He added this comment, "For if ye forgive men their trespasses, your heavenly Father will also forgive you: but if ye forgive not men their trespasses, neither will your Father forgive your trespasses" (Matthew 6:14,15).

Four

Those Feelings
of Rejection

Great joy comes in realizing that you have been of service to somebody. That joy is experienced by a parent, a physician, a minister, a teacher, by every person in society, because in one way or another every person does something to help somebody else. As we look back over our lives we remember with real satisfaction the services we have been privileged to render to other people. Even Jesus had that feeling. One of the saddest stories in all of literature is the one about Jesus healing the ten lepers. All ten of them came asking His help and all ten were healed. Jesus saw the needs of those ten people who were afflicted with the dread disease of leprosy, and He had compassion for them. He brought about their healing. Then we read:

> And one of them, when he saw that he was healed, turned back, and with a loud voice glorified God, and fell down on his face at his feet, giving him thanks: and he was a Samaritan.
>
> (Luke 17:15,16)

Any one of us can share something of the feeling Jesus had in the expression of thanks He received from that grateful man. During the times when we are experiencing sadness and loneliness, one of the things that gives us inspiration is thinking about people who have expressed appreciation to us.

And now come those very, very sad lines—"And Jesus answering said, Were there not ten cleansed? But where are the nine?"(v. 17).

Many of us can identify with another scene in the life of Jesus, when Jesus was extremely popular and great crowds followed Him. On this occasion five thousand people went with Him out into the wilderness. Lunchtime came and there was nothing to eat. Then Jesus took the five loaves of bread and two fishes that a little boy gave Him and performed a miracle in feeding those five thousand. The people were gloriously excited and some of them even wanted to make Him a king. But He explained to them that providing physical bread was not His greatest mission in life; rather He had come to minister to their souls. He also explained that sacrifices would be required of those who follow Him. Then we read, "From that time many of his disciples went back, and walked no more with him" (John 6:66).

Sometimes in life we think that the only reason someone may want us is for what they can get out of us. Then, when it seems that they can get more someplace else or from somebody else, they drop us. Being rejected is a difficult thing.

Jesus went with His disciples to the Garden of Gethsemane and there He separated Himself a little from them to pray. He asked His disciples to be on the watch while He prayed. However, they went to sleep. When He came back from that very difficult ordeal and saw His disciples asleep He said, "What, could ye not watch with me one hour?" (Matthew 26:40). In that time of great crisis, the ones He counted on and depended on seemed to desert Him. He had a feeling of being let down by His closest loved ones.

Still another scene in the life of Jesus comes to mind. As He was on the cross His pain was so bitter, the disappointment was so great, and the people had been so cruel that He felt deserted not only by His friends but even by His heavenly Father. He cried, "My God, my God, why hast thou forsaken me?" (Mark 15:34). That was the only time that Jesus ever referred to God as God. In every other instance He spoke of His dear "Father." Perhaps in that moment of pain and disapointment, He felt that even His Father had deserted Him.

In counseling with many people across the years who were going through the difficulties of readjusting after a divorce, I often found this very feeling. Over and over I have heard, "After what I did for him or her, I was not appreciated. . . ." Sometimes, in moments of great stress and strain, we come to feel that even God has deserted us.

We hear a lot about people in the world who are physically hungry. One of the great tragedies throughout the centuries has been starving people. However, a hungry heart can be an even greater burden than an empty stomach.

Through the years my phone has always been listed so that people could call me day or night. I never permitted my secretary, when taking a call, to ask who is calling. I was willing to talk to whoever called and if that caller did not want to reveal his or her identity that was fine with me.

Not long ago a young lady called saying she would like to talk with me. I assured her that I had time and was happy for us to talk. She told me that at the time of her birth her mother developed complications and died. When she was two years old her father died. She was taken to live with relatives who felt obligated to take care of her, but who obviously felt she was an intrusion into their lives. She was made to feel unwanted. When she was fifteen years old she moved to the city and got a job with a large company, and for seventeen years now, she has worked for this large company. She was living in a boarding house and had almost no friends or companions. She said, "I do not know what it means to be loved by one person one time."

Deep in every heart there is a yearning to be accepted, to be loved, and to have a feeling that you mean something to somebody.

Before Samuel Liebowitz became a judge in New York City he was a defense lawyer in criminal cases. In talking about his life he told of defending seventy-eight accused murderers, every one of whom he saved from the electric chair. Then he said, "Not one of them ever bothered to even send me a Christmas card."

Years ago a man named Art King established what he called a "Job Center of the Air." Over the radio, people would call in and tell him about the jobs they were seeking. During the years of that program he was able to help twenty-five hundred people find good positions. But after he had discontinued the program he said, "Only ten ever thanked me."

Even Abraham Lincoln had some of this feeling. In his very first speech when running for public office he said to the voters, "I have no other ambition so great as that of being truly esteemed by my fellow man."

After Napoleon Bonaparte was exiled on St. Helena, shut away from all the people he had known, one of the last things he said before he died was, "I should very much like to know whether Herr Bauer ever learned how I made good." Herr Bauer was one of his early schoolteachers who had somehow made the little boy Napoleon feel slighted, rejected, and unappreciated. All his life Napoleon had carried in his heart the wound of being slighted by that teacher.

It was Helen Hunt Jackson who said, "If you love me, tell me that you love me; the realm of silence is large enough beyond the grave."

I was counseling with a man one day when, in talking about his wife and children, he said, and these are his exact words:

"Their hands are constantly held out to receive, but so help me God, not once a year do I get one word of appreciation. Couldn't one of them, just one—just one mind you—break down and say, 'Gee, Dad, that was swell of you.' "

John Steinbeck wrote, in *East of Eden*, "I think everyone in the world to a large or small extent has felt rejection. And with rejection comes anger, with anger comes some kind of crime in revenge for the rejection, and with the crime comes guilt."

Sometimes one is tempted to say as Shakespeare said—"Ingratitude, thou marble-hearted fiend!"

An author worked long and hard in writing a play which he hoped to see produced on the stage. He carried it to publisher after publisher and it was rejected by every one. Finally he gave up. "This has been a case of all work and no play," he said.

A minister was walking through one of the new-made American cemeteries in France after the first world war when he saw a mother weeping over a grave. Going over to her he said, "Madame, you have my sympathy."

The woman looked up and answered, "I do not want your sympathy."

Somewhat taken aback, the minister answered, "Well, you have it whether you want it or not."

The woman then said, "No, I do not want your sympathy; I do not ask for your prayers. What I want is your appreciation."

When one feels that he or she has given an awful lot to a marriage and now the marriage is broken—then one may need some sympathy, but that one also wants some appreciation.

Five

Worry
and Fear

Today many of us live in the most affluent society the world has ever known. We have developed all sorts of mechanical gadgets to make life easier and more interesting and we are the best fed, clothed, and housed people of history. Yet in our society today there are more suicides than ever before, more people in mental hospitals, more people taking drugs.

Albert Camus, a brilliant Frenchman, called this "the century of fear." Another refers to it as "the age of anxiety."

Read the novels and the plays being written today, look at the

motion pictures and many of the television programs, listen to
the popular songs—many of these are about unhappy, fear-rid-
den people who can't find any answers to life.

Especially do these upsetting feelings come to one who has
been through some traumatic experience—especially an unhappy
divorce; and no matter what the circumstances or the reasons,
nearly every divorce is unhappy.

The basic cause of anxiety is the fear that we will be forced
into a situation that we cannot handle. We're afraid that the circumstances we are facing in life will overwhelm us.

There are many reasons for marrying, but one of the fruits of
marriage is a feeling of security. We have somebody who is our
companion, who will love us, who will take care of us in a time of
need—in every situation of life the one to whom I am married
will be there by my side. Then, we realize that that one is not by
our side anymore and it is not easy to get used to being alone
again.

When I think of fear, anxiety, moving out into a new life, and
all that it involves, my mind goes back to one of the most dramatic stories in all of history. It is the story about Moses dividing
the Red Sea for the children of Israel to pass through out of
bondage into their promised land. For ten generations the children of Israel had been slaves in a foreign land. Life for them was
filled with ceaseless toil.

Many nights, they gathered around the hearthstones of their
crude cabins and heard stories of the faith of their ancestors—
they learned about Abraham, about Isaac and Jacob, and about
Joseph. They maintained the altars of faith; they continued to
believe in the power of God. They never gave up their dreams of
their "promised land." Someday they would be free again.

There was a man by the name of Moses who had ruled over
them, who had become one of them, and then had disappeared.
Now he was back again demanding freedom for his people. "Let
my people go," he demanded of Pharaoh. Moses had a strange
and wonderful power. Even the great Pharaoh could not stand
up to him. The day finally arrived when the Israelites packed

their belongings and were on their way toward the land that "flowed with milk and honey."

Freedom was now theirs but actually their anxieties and their fears and their worries were just beginning. In slavery, they had enjoyed a certain kind of security. They knew they would have a place to sleep and some food to eat. Now they were on their own. Would they be able to find their way through the wilderness? Would they have enough food to live on? Would the promised land be as good as they hoped?

Curiously, anxiety is not only born out of adversity; it also results from blessings which we fear we may lose. Many times the most blessed people are the most anxious people.

As the children of Israel journeyed toward the realization of their dreams, the word came that Pharaoh had changed his mind about letting them go free. With his armies, the hated dictator was now after them. They hurried their pace. They would break camp early in the morning and they would march longer into the night. Maybe they could keep ahead of the dreaded Pharaoh.

Then came that dreadful day when they arrived at the sea. There it stretched before them to block their path. They had no boats. They could go no farther. They had no weapons to fight the army pursuing them. There was no hope either forward or backward. They seemed doomed in their helplessness.

Now comes one of the grandest scenes in the entire Bible. I am not referring to the dividing of the Red Sea. To see the waters roll back and the dry land appear, providing a pathway to safety, was truly a dramatically wonderful experience. But that was really the anticlimax. Even more wonderful was what happened before the sea was divided. In the midst of their anguished disappointment, Moses stood up. He got their attention and this is what he said:

"Fear ye not, stand still, and see the salvation of the Lord, which he will show to you today: for the Egyptians whom ye have seen today, ye shall see them again no more forever. The Lord shall fight for you, and ye shall hold your peace" (Exodus 14:13, 14).

What a marvelous faith Moses had! These people had been in such a hurry, packing up their belongings, moving out, traveling day by day, that they had forgotten there was help for them beyond their own resources. Notice that Moses said to the people, "Stand still." We remember how the psalmist said, "Be still, and know that I am God" (Psalms 46:10). One of the greatest needs of people is to learn how to be quiet. One of our greatest sins is being in too big of a hurry.

Why did Moses want the people to stand still? He gives the answer, "to see the salvation of the Lord." In times of anxious fear, we need to realize that there are forces beyond human strength that come to help us. We come to these places in life when it seems like we can't go back and we can't go forward. We seem stuck and we become panicky.

For many years I have quoted a poem that I think is wonderful. It is one of the best and finest poems I know about. And it suits our discussion of the Hebrew deliverance.

> *Have you come to the Red Sea place in your life,*
> *Where, in spite of all you can do*
> *There is no way out, there is no way back,*
> *There is no other way but—through?*
> *Then wait on the Lord with a trust serene,*
> *Till the night of your fear is gone;*
> *He will send the wind, He will heap the floods*
> *He says to your soul, "Go on."*
>
> *And His hand will lead you through—clear through—*
> *Ere the watery walls roll down.*
> *No foe can reach you, no wave can touch,*
> *No mightiest sea can drown;*
> *The tossing billows may rear their crests,*
> *Their foam at your feet may break;*
> *But over their bed you shall walk dry shod,*
> *In a path that your Lord will make.*
>
> *In the morning watch, 'neath the lifted cloud,*
> *You shall see but the Lord alone,*

Where He leads you on from the place by the sea
To the land that you have not known;
And your fears shall pass as your foes have passed,
You shall be no more afraid.
You shall sing His praise in another place,
In a place that His hand has made.

                                        Annie Johnson Flint

I speak often of the stained-glass windows in the sanctuary of Grace United Methodist Church in Atlanta, Georgia. When I was pastor of that church some years ago, those windows were created and placed in the church; and I found great inspiration in them. The climax of the windows is the one over the choir, behind the pulpit. It is the one directly before the people while they are assembled in worship. It shows the ascension of Christ, the time when the Lord is leaving His disciples and saying to them that He is putting this work into their hands and they are to be responsible for it. He had commanded them, "Go ye into all the world" (Mark 16:15). Surely this was a frightening time for these disciples. They had found strength in being in the presence of Christ. They had seen Him perform mighty and wonderful miracles. They had heard Him speak to great multitudes of people in most convincing ways.

Now, His work was on their shoulders. They had to go out alone. They would not have the strengthening support of Christ. Surely it was a very difficult moment for them.

More than half of that window that depicts the Ascension is deep blue sky. Looking at the window, some people have said there was too much blue in it. But the artist knew what he was doing when he made it that way.

Psychologists who have made a careful study of the effects of color on the human spirit have learned that the color blue reduces tension, lowers blood pressure, stabilizes heart action, and relieves anxiety more than any other color. The color blue creates an atmosphere in which one can more easily throw off the worries of life.

Dr. Norman Vincent Peale, the minister in America who has blessed my life the most and whose friendship continues to be a joy and a strength to me, tells about his conversation with the man who repairs the windows in the ancient Cathedral of Chartres in France. This man told him that the one color that has not disintegrated under the elements during the centuries is the blue of the ancient craftsmen. He declared that the reason Chartres is so stimulating to the human spirit is because of the deep blues which the light filters.

The main point I am making is this—if the color through which we look at the light influences our minds and spirits, how much greater are we influenced by the windows through which we look at life. Moses said, "Stand still, and see the salvation of the Lord." That is—first get God in your mind and then look at your problems through the windows of your faith. Color your thinking with God and your anxiety will cease to dominate you.

Some time ago I was talking in my office with a man who was very disturbed. I suggested to him that instead of talking about his difficult problem that we set aside exactly one minute—sixty seconds—and do as I suggested. He agreed. I said to him something like this, "Now let your body be as relaxed as possible. Think of God as being right there by your side. Think of God's power flowing into you. Think of God opening the way through these problems of your life. Picture in your mind the dividing of the Red Sea and realize that God can provide a pathway along which you can walk through your difficult problems to the other side. Feel deep peace possessing your mind. Now say with Moses, 'The Lord shall fight for me, and I shall hold my peace.' "

I suggest to the readers of this page that when you feel you've come to the "Red Sea place" in your life you do for one minute what I asked that friend of mine to do. Many times you will feel marvelous results.

"To worry about what we can't help is useless," someone has said. "To worry about what we can help is stupid."

Some of us would do well to emulate the woman who realized that her fears were ruining her life, so she made for herself a "worry

table." In tabulating her worries, she discovered these figures:
40 percent will never happen; anxiety is the result of a tired mind.

30 percent are about old decisions which I cannot alter.

12 percent represent others' criticism of me, most of which is untrue made by people who feel inferior.

10 percent are about my health, which gets worse as I worry.

8 percent are "legitimate," since life has some real problems to meet.

"Our main business is not to see what lies dimly in the distance, but to do what lies clearly at hand," said Thomas Carlyle.

᛫ "Let us be of good cheer, remembering that the misfortunes hardest to bear are those which never happen," said James Russell Lowell.

In her book, *My Heart Shall Not Fear,* Josephine Lawrence offers these insightful words: " 'It sounds to me as if you might be more afraid of living than of dying,' Emmeline said. 'Nicholas is growing like a weed, and the real question is what you are going to do with his life and yours.' She removed her glasses to polish them with her handkerchief; without them her face looked unfamiliar and strained. 'Maybe I'd better tell you what it's taken me eighty years to learn,' she suggested. 'Please, grandmother.'

"The glasses slipped back into place, and a wise, shrewd, old lady peered out. 'You might write it down and hang it in your new apartment, where you'll see it every morning,' Emmeline said. 'It's only five words long, but each one counts: DON'T LET LIFE SCARE YOU—that's all.' "

"What is a budget?" someone asked.

"Well, it is a method of worrying before you spend instead of afterward." Worry is the interest you pay on trouble before it comes.

"The best cure for worry, depression, melancholy, or brooding, is to go deliberately forth and try to lift with one's sympathy, the gloom of somebody else," said Arnold Bennett.

"He who reigns within himself and rules his passions, desires, and fears, is more than a king," said Milton.

Worry is an old man with bended head,
Carrying a load of feathers
Which he thinks are lead.

                              Author unknown

"Without God, we cannot. Without us, God will not" (St. Augustine).

Six

Making a Hard Decision _____

There is an old story about a man who hired out to a farmer. His job the first day was cutting wood. He worked hard. The second day the farmer put the man out in the field to dig weeds. The sun was hot but the man threw himself vigorously into the work. The third day it was raining, so the farmer had the man sort potatoes in the barn. It was easy work; all he had to do was look at each potato and put the rotten ones in one pile and the good ones in another pile. At noon the man told the farmer he was quitting. The farmer was amazed. He said, "The first day you worked hard cutting wood, the second day you dug weeds.

Now I give you a nice easy job and you quit. Why?" The man
replied, "I didn't mind the work, but when I started sorting potatoes, I couldn't stand to make those decisions."

As we go along through life, we don't mind the work; but the
hardest part of living is the making of decisions. That is where
most of our failures are—not that we make bad decisions, but
rather that we often are unable to decide at all. We remember
how Elijah said to the people, "How long halt ye between two
opinions? if the Lord be God, follow him: but if Baal, then follow
him." Now comes one of the saddest lines in the Bible: "And the
people answered him not a word" (1 Kings 18:21). They
wouldn't say yes; they wouldn't say no. They just wouldn't say.

We remember the classic story of the donkey standing between two haystacks. The hay was fragrant and the donkey was
hungry. Yet he could never decide which stack to turn to. When
he was minded to feast off one, the delightful aroma of the other
tantalized him. And so it went until, according to the story, the
poor donkey stood between the two haystacks and finally starved
to death.

That represents a lot of people—people who have never
learned to make up their minds. The greatest enemy to life is in-
decision. When facing some hard decision, take a good look at
Pilate. He was faced with the most important decision of all time:
"What shall I do then with Jesus . . . ?" (Matthew 27:22). We all
have that decision to make. We have other decisions, too, and it
will help us to see Pilate's problems and the mistakes he made in
arriving at his decision.

Pilate was the Roman governor of Judea. Early one morning,
a mob brought Jesus before him to be tried. Pilate really had no
interest in the case; yet he was young and ambitious and he
wanted to take no chances on his own future. He already had had
trouble with the people and exciting them further might have
endangered his position. On the other hand, he had a conscience
and a sense of justice. No matter what his decision might be, it
would likely cause trouble. So, when faced with a hard decision,
Pilate lost out on the greatest chance of his life because he didn't
know how to make up his mind.

I have often wondered what the last two thousand years might have been if only Pilate had had the courage of his convictions. Without his permission, Jesus could not have been crucified. Instead of dying at the age of thirty-three, He might have lived to be seventy-three or even eighty-three. Suppose the Lord had lived for forty or fifty more years on this earth? What a difference it might have made!

And Pilate really did not want to see Him crucified. Pilate's was probably the friendliest face Jesus saw at all His trials. "I find in him no fault at all," Pilate said (John 18:38); but he was "on the spot." To release Him would have offended the people, maybe getting him in trouble with Rome and thwarting his personal ambitions. It would have been the popular thing to let Him be crucified.

On the other hand, there was something mysterious about Christ that troubled Pilate. During the trial that morning, a message came from Claudia, Pilate's wife, saying, "Have thou nothing to do with that just man: for I have suffered many things this day in a dream because of him" (Matthew 27:19).

It is possible that Claudia had come to know Jesus. Maybe one day, as she passed through the city, she had seen Him lifting some crippled man off his bed; maybe she had paused as He was speaking and listened to His wonderful words; maybe their eyes had met as they chanced to pass on the street; maybe one of her servants had told her about Jesus. Someone has well said:

> *I did but see him passing by,*
> *And yet I'll love him till I die.*

Maybe Claudia was interceding for Him; or maybe she had had a dream and was frightened at what might happen, and Pilate shared that fright. Certainly he did not want to make the decision concerning Jesus.

I find it in my heart to condemn Pilate, but before I do I must point out that we too have important decisions to make. And in condemning Pilate, we condemn ourselves. Instead of facing up to his responsibility, Pilate began to run from his decision.

Evasion

First he tried to evade a decision. He said, "Take ye him, and judge him . . ." (John 18:31); that is, put the responsibility on the crowd. We do that many times when faced with some decision of life. Instead of determining our own course, we say, "Everybody else is doing it, I'll follow the crowd." But that never satisfies, and it didn't work in Pilate's case. Pilate sent Jesus to Herod (Luke 23:7); he tried to put the decision on somebody else. But Herod sent Him back. We can never evade our own responsibility. I have had many people come to me for counseling on problems, but one thing I have learned: you cannot make someone else's decision for him. Pilate made one more effort at evasion: he tried to substitute Barabbas. Instead of squarely facing the issue, we bring up some other issue and evade the main one.

Compromise

When faced with a hard decision, we often seek to compromise with it if we cannot evade it. When Pilate faced the question, "What then shall I do with Jesus?" he did not want to crucify Him; yet it would have caused trouble if he had let Him go. So Pilate took a middle course. He wouldn't say yes and wouldn't say no.

The Bible says, "Then Pilate therefore took Jesus, and scourged him" (John 19:1). Then said Pilate, "Behold the man!"(v. 5). He was saying, "Hasn't His suffering now been enough?" But the crowd was not satisfied. Nobody is ever satisfied with compromise. They shouted, "Crucify him . . ." (v. 6). Now Pilate had lost his chance. James Russell Lowell was right when he said:

> Once to every man and nation comes the moment to decide, . . .
> And the choice goes by forever 'twixt the darkness and the light.

Decisions have a way of not waiting, and if we evade and compromise, decisions move on out of our reach and we are left behind in defeat. No one has ever put it better than Shakespeare:

There is a tide in the affairs of men,
Which, taken at the flood, leads on to fortune;
Omitted, all the voyage of their life
Is bound in shallows and in miseries.

Then Pilate dramatically "took water, and washed his hands before the multitude, saying, I am innocent of the blood of this just person: see ye to it" (Matthew 27:24). It would be wonderful if we could evade our hard decisions and then simply wash our hands of them. But such is never the case. We have a responsibility for many things and we must accept the responsibility of our decisions. The world has never let Pilate loose from his decision. I am persuaded that God never let him off, either. But also he couldn't let himself off; he had to live with his failure the balance of his days.

I don't know what Pilate's life was after that day, but we may rest assured that he was never a real man again. His failure to decide tore away the inner strengths of his soul and left him a defeated coward. Over His cross Pilate put the words, "Jesus of Nazareth, the King of the Jews" (John 19:19). The people wanted the sign changed but he stubbornly refused, saying, "What I have written, I have written" (v. 22). He might have changed the inscription, but what he said applied to his own life. Opportunities come; we make some decision, saying yes or no, or we run away from the decision. Whatever—

The Moving Finger writes; and, having writ,
Moves on. . . .

There is a legend that Pilate, like Judas, found life unbearable. Instead of hanging himself, he tried to run away and eventually got to Switzerland. There he drowned himself in a lake, and the legend is that on moonlight nights one can see the ghost of Pilate, forever moaning, forever washing his hands. Whether the legend is true does not matter. What is true is that the universe offers no place to retreat from the reality of life. No matter what the cost, better for Pilate had he made the right decision. So it is for me—for you.

* * *

Consider the most disappointing moment in a baseball game. If you love baseball, you like to see the batter get a hit, or a fielder make an outstanding play. You can accept it when one of the players makes an error; and you know that the team you are cheering for is going to lose a game from time to time. You come to accept all this. What is hard to accept is a batter being called out with his bat on his shoulder. I can understand a batter striking out; but I like for him to swing at the ball and at least give himself a chance.

So it is in life. We are going to make some unwise decisions, but at least let's give ourselves a chance. Let's not strike out with our bat on our shoulder.

"If you want a strong life," said Ernest Poole in *One of Us,* "you must learn to pick and choose, and not putter around with details."

When Antiochus of Syria invaded Egypt, the Romans sent a herald, Pompilius, to order him to withdraw. After Pompilius delivered the message, Antiochus read it and said, "I will consider the matter and answer soon." The herald then took his wand, the symbol of his office, and drew a circle around Antiochus and replied, "Consider and answer before you step out of the circle."

In moments when a decision is required, maybe it would be good to draw a circle around ourselves.

Count von Moltke, the German strategist and general, chose for his motto, *"Erst wägen, dann wagen"* (First weigh—then venture").

The great Augustine prayed, "Lord, save me from my sins, but not quite yet."

Sometime after that he prayed, "Lord, save me from all my sins, except one."

Then came the final prayer: "Lord, save me from all my sins, and save me now!"

Sometimes we feel that we are completely defeated, that everything is going against us; we can see no hope. Then it is that we remember the words of Henry Wadsworth Longfellow, "The lowest ebb is the turn of the tide."

Seven

Children and Divorce _____

The overwhelming majority of the couples who obtain a divorce have no children. Many of the others have only one child. For some this would seem to suggest that the alarm about divorce affecting children has been greatly exaggerated.

However, for the divorced parents with children, this is a very important concern and should be addressed. While divorce is a method of ending a personal relationship, when children are involved, their relationship to their parents is not ended. That child is still the child of its father and mother. Even though the marriage was not good for the parent, it is very likely that the marriage met the needs of the child as the parents carried out their roles as mother and father, even though the husband-wife roles were suffering.

Of course, divorce affects children of various ages differently. Infants adjust very quickly; children up to three years old may have some immediate problems which create excessive crying and difficulties in sleeping. However, these young children usually overcome their problems rather quickly and have few long lasting problems of adjustment.

Children between the ages of three and six are usually rather distressed and upset by divorce. They are frightened because one of their parents is not with them, and they have no understanding of the reason for a divorce; but they recognize that something has happened. This child cannot understand why a parent would leave if he or she loved the family.

This age child has rather difficult emotional problems resulting from divorce. The preschool-age child probably has more difficulty with divorce than children of any other age. They have lost the assurance that their parents would always be with them and they become fearful, having lost one parent, that they may eventually lose the other parent and be left alone. Also, the preschool-age child has more of a tendency to blame himself. This is the age when a child is corrected often and, having done something to be corrected for, may subconsciously feel that he or she caused the parents to separate.

The school-aged child is much better able to understand his parents' explanations. This child can be very negatively affected by a divorce and his confidence can be greatly shaken. This age child is much more likely to pit one parent against the other.

As children grow older they demonstrate their feelings more openly. Oftentimes they are very critical of their parents and go through a period of, "I do not love either of you anymore." The teenager, having a better understanding of what a family means, suffers a greater loss. A teenager's dreams of family life and family love and family security are shaken and, many times, they are not very sympathetic toward divorcing parents. Or they take sides with one parent against the other. Teens also are more responsive to the opinions of their peers and they feel looked down upon at times after their home has suffered that traumatic experience.

Not only does divorce often create a feeling of insecurity; it also brings about a sense of being ashamed. If a child's parent dies, that child knows it has the sympathy and love of other people. When a divorce has happened, the child can feel that somebody was at fault. Oftentimes before the divorce, the marriage has been shaky and the child, in many cases, has already experienced feelings of rejection and insecurity. Then the divorce happens and those feelings are greater because now the situation seems hopeless.

Divorce is not something a child gets over quickly. In fact, very possibly a child never gets over it. Not only is the child's faith in his or her parents' marriage completely broken, but as the child grows older it has less faith in marriage itself and may fear that his or her own marriage might also fail.

Children desperately need to maintain contact with both parents. Usually in a divorce one parent is given custody of the child. Many people who have studied children of divorced parents are very strong in their opinion that when the child has a good relationship with both parents then the child survives the crisis much, much better.

The best and most concise suggestions I have ever read with reference to dealing with children are these words written by Cecil Murphey in *The Encyclopedia for Today's Christian Woman:*

1. Tell the Truth. Children generally know when you're lying or trying to hold back. They don't need to know everything (and shouldn't), but they do need to know basic facts.
2. Expect to Feel Ambivalent About the Children. For the custodial parent, a heavy weight often hangs on them. At times you may think or perhaps even say out loud, "If I didn't have children to tie me down, I could. . . ." With almost the next breath you'll probably add, "But my

children enrich my life. The problems are worth it, just to have them."

Those feelings are natural. Most custodial parents go through it. Try to accept those feelings as normal.

3. Having Custody Doesn't Prevent Loneliness. "At least I have my son," one mother recalls saying shortly after the marital breakup. "For the first few weeks we had so many adjustments to make, I didn't think about being lonely. But after a while, it got to me. I had almost no adult companionship. I wanted to talk about anything adult—recipes, books, morality, theology. But how much of that can you do with a five-year-old?"

4. Being the Custodial Parent Means No Other Parent There to Undercut Authority. In family stress, one parent tends to allow the youngsters to break the rules the other has set. If you have custody, you set the rules and you enforce them. (When they visit the other parent and the rules change, they still need to know what to expect when with you.)

5. You'll Never Have Enough Time With Your Children. If you're the custodial parent, it generally means you're also working. One mother said, "In trying to be both mother and father, you never have enough time for your children. You're too busy doing things for them—especially when they're young. But you have so little time to hold them, to love them, or simply to listen."

6. Allow the Children to Express Their Emotions Over the Divorce—both at the time they hear about it and later. They have a right to their moods and depressions just as the parents do. If they scream and say they hate you, allow it. Let them use any nondestructive outlet. And let them know it's okay to feel the way they do.

7. Tell Your Children They Didn't Cause the Divorce. Many children blame themselves. "I was naughty and Daddy left" or, "I'm not nice and my parents split up." The feelings of guilt are never logical. But the child may need assurance that he or she was not the factor in the divorce.

8. Explain the Future to the Children. As much as possible let them know where they'll live, what will happen in school. Tell them of the lowered standard of living. Also let them know how often they can expect to see the other parent.

Most of all, give them a sense of security and help them feel that life is under control.

9. Don't Allow the Children to Play the "Parent Trap" Game. Don't encourage them to plot ways to get mother and father back together. When the divorce becomes final, don't hold up the possibility of reconciliation. If there is a possibility (and not merely a vague hope), be honest there, too.

10. Don't Get Overly Concerned About the Broken-Home Image. As stated earlier, one-parent families can be as happy and healthy as two-parent families. In fact, when children grow up in an atmosphere of being loved and feeling secure, the actual circumstances make little difference.

11. Be a Parent, Not a Buddy, and Not a Brother or Sister. Your child can develop friendships. They can't easily find parents. They need authority figures to set the limits for their behavior.

12. Don't Expect Too Much From the Children. Don't make the oldest the housekeeper or a surrogate mate. Or don't go to the opposite extreme of being overly protective and sheltering. Don't give your children the picture of "you and me against the world."

13. If Your Children Show Serious Behavioral or Emotional Problems, Get Help. Single parents often wonder, will my son turn into a homosexual if he's only around females? Or will my daughter become promiscuous? If this troubles you, get help. If you're a mother, find surrogate fathers for your son.

14. As a Christian Parent, Remember Your Responsibilities Before God. Most believers either have their children baptized or dedicated. That presentation of children is also a covenant with God. As a parent you promise your faithfulness to teach your children about Him. Even though your marriage has dissolved and you may personally be in heavy turmoil, keep the children's lives as natural as possible.

Keep involved in your congregation.

If you're not already doing so, I suggest you pray for and with your children every day. Let them know your concern.

Have a daily Bible reading plan. Those few minutes communicate to your children that you consider God an important aspect of life.

15. Most Important, Let the Children Know You Love Them. You can show your love in hundreds of ways. Take time to listen to the children when they want to talk. If you can't stop then, why not say, "Sammy, I'm very busy right now, but as soon as I finish, I'll sit down and we'll talk." Then keep that promise.

Let them know where you are. They may never need to call, but it gives them a sense of security to know that you can be reached if they need you. That includes when you go out on dates, too.

Don't hesitate to tell them that you love them. Especially in the months after the divorce, the children need to hear that often. Don't assume they know because you pay the bills or take them places. They need to have it expressed.

We need to experience human love, too.

Eight

Alone in the Crowd _____

A good many people go through life single. In these pages, however, we are thinking of those who were once married, and have become single again. Our adult society is made up of singles and marrieds. But many of the people who have been divorced have difficulty believing they belong to either group. They think of themselves as married, and yet they are single. Their whole mental attitude is toward the married life, but now they must learn to live the single life. That is a very difficult adjustment to make, and many people never really make it.

They remember parties and other social events when as a couple they were invited, but now somehow their names get left off some of the invitation lists. It is not easy to think about dear friends having a party and you being left out. Even if you go to the party, being a single you feel uncomfortable with the marrieds.

Even though a divorced parent has children, that does not completely fill the void. There is joy in being with children, but there are times when people really need some relationships with their peers.

If one has a job, of course that helps both to fulfill some of the purposes of life and also gives one relationships with others. But there is a difference between work relationships and social relationships. One may be encouraged to develop hobby and recreational activities, but doing those things alone oftentimes is not very much fun.

Loneliness takes many forms. There is the loneliness of the midnight hour when all is quiet. There is the loneliness that Robinson Crusoe felt on an uninhabited island. There is the loneliness one might feel far out in the desert.

I was interested once to hear a man talk about his feelings after he had climbed to the top of a very high mountain. It was quite a struggle to reach that peak and finally he did. As he stood on the top, he felt an indescribable loneliness.

That same principle works in life. Many who have struggled to the very top of their profession, or have become famous or quite wealthy, find themselves very lonely. Feeling lonely and depressed, they might look around and see how well off they are. They may have a nice place to live in and plenty to eat and clothes to wear and a car to drive and financial security; they might have accomplished outstanding things in their lives. Even so, their blessings and achievements do not overcome their loneliness.

More and more people in our society are discovering the loneliness of the city. In small towns everybody knows everybody and, in a sense, everybody is a part of everybody. In large cities, however, we see many, many people who are hurrying hither and yon in their respective endeavors. They are like you and me. They have passions, hopes, fears, joys, and sorrows. But they are really not a part of the society around them.

Never shall I forget a banquet at which a very prominent person had been given an outstanding award. After the banquet was over, I was congratulating him and he said to me, "I appreciate this honor, but it really doesn't mean much to me now. My wife died last year and now when I go home I have nobody to tell it to."

Joys which cannot be shared are really not very joyful. Sorrows, when there is no one to sympathize, are much more difficult to bear. Surely there must have been a tear in the eye of the psalmist when he wrote, "No man cared for my soul" (Psalms 142:4).

In the story of the Creation, the Bible tells us, "And the Lord God said, It is not good that the man should be alone; I will make him an help meet for him" (Genesis 2:18). After one has been divorced finding someone else to marry at that moment may not be the major concern; but having been part of a marriage relationship, and now being single, one not only is caused to feel lonely. It is a very unnatural and even frightening situation.

This feeling of being "on the ouside," isolated, alienated, is one of the heavy burdens of divorce. André Gide said that people suffer from "the fear of finding themselves alone so they don't find themselves at all." After the breakup of a love relationship, many people do not feel sorrow or humiliation so much as they feel "empty." One person explained that the loss of a marriage partner leaves "an inner yawning void."

Carl Sandburg pointed out that William Shakespeare, Leonardo da Vinci, Benjamin Franklin, and Lincoln never saw a movie, heard a radio or looked at TV. They experienced loneliness and knew what to do with it. They were not afraid of being lonely because they knew that was when the creative mood in them would work.

However, many of us do not feel that we are a Shakespeare,

a da Vinci, a Franklin, or a Lincoln; many times normal people
have real difficulties in knowing what to do with loneliness.

Hardly a week passes but that I receive at least one letter from
someone who has read my book, *You Are Never Alone*. In that
book about loneliness and what to do about it, I told the following story:

> Sometime ago I was talking with a very distin-
> guished minister who is now retired. He told me that
> he is eighty-seven years old, and ever since he learned
> to read he has read at least one chapter of the Bible
> every day. Most days he reads several chapters. He
> had read entirely through the Bible a number of
> times. I asked him, "Havng spent so much time read-
> ing the Scriptures, what is the one verse that you
> would pick out as your favorite?"
>
> I could hardly wait to hear his answer. Here was a
> man who had lived more than eighty years with the
> Bible, who knew it, as the saying goes, "from cover to
> cover." He hesitated about replying. (During that
> time I thought of several of my own favorite Bible
> verses. I was trying to decide which one particular
> verse I would say is my favorite.) Finally he said to
> me, "You will find my favorite Bible verse fifteen or
> twenty times, scattered through the Bible." He said,
> "And it came to pass . . ." (Exodus 12:41, Acts 27:44
> and many other places).
>
> I really was shocked and disappointed. I said, "Do
> you mean to tell me that—in all the Bible—that one
> dangling phrase, 'And it came to pass,' is your favorite
> verse?"
>
> As he answered me, I felt like I was being rebuked.
> "Let me tell you that there is no verse in the Bible
> that can help you more than this." He went on, "I
> have lived long enough to know the truth of that
> phrase, 'It came to pass.' All the miseries of life come

to pass. Even the joys of life come to pass. All the heartaches, the troubles, the wars, the crime—all come to pass.

"A baby is born in your home, but the baby grows up and becomes a man or woman. It came to pass. You have your job, your work in life, but it came to pass. You marry and live with someone whom you love more than you love yourself—but it came to pass. There is an old song entitled 'Count Your Many Blessings,' but they all 'came to pass.' "

I started thinking about some of the happenings in my own life that I worried about—some of the events that I felt were very hurtful and that maybe I would not get over. Now, as I look back, I realize, "It came to pass." I thought about some of the occurrences that I thought were of the utmost importance, but now they are not important at all. They "came to pass."

This also applies to so many delightful and pleasurable experiences. We need to learn how to enjoy what we have when we can enjoy them, because all of the pleasures of life eventually "come to pass."

If today you feel heavy burdens and heartache—if you feel that tomorrow is hopeless—if you feel that you do not have the resources, the strengths to make it in life—just remember, "It came to pass." Nothing came to stay. Tomorrow will be a new day with a new chance, new strengths, and new opportunity. If you can really believe "it came to pass," then all despair in your life can somehow be taken away.

"It came to pass."

Nine

Divorce Is a New Beginning

At the very start let us settle in our minds the religious issues with reference to divorce and remarriage. We hear many ideas and opinions expressed on this subject. Certainly, in a complex society such as ours we are never going to come to unanimity on this subject. If we were to poll all the people in one particular church we would find that they vary greatly in their views. Even if we could get a bus load of American ministers to discuss it, they would never all agree. In fact, a bus load of ministers of the same denomination would not reach a unanimous opinion. Sincere and religious people disagree on this subject.

There are those who say that it is acceptable to remarry if a marriage and divorce take place prior to spiritual salvation. They quote 2 Corinthians 5:17: "Therefore, if any man be in Christ, he is a new creature; old things are passed away; behold, all things are become new." The idea here is that after spiritual salvation people become fresh, restored, new creatures. That is, they are forgiven.

Certainly it is within the power of God's loving mercy to wipe the slate clean of our past mistakes. However, there are obligations that "salvation" does not cancel. For example, if I owe a note at the bank, I could not go to the bank and say that I have recently become "saved" and therefore want them to cancel my debt. The bank would not accept that.

A justifiable reason for divorce cited by many people is immorality on the part of one of the marriage partners. We read in Matthew 19:9, "And I say unto you, Whosoever shall put away his wife, except it be for fornication, and shall marry another, committeth adultery; and whoso marrieth her which is put away doth commit adultery." Some interpret this to mean that if one of the partners has a "one-time-only," divorce is justified. Others suggest that this refers to a prolonged period of unfaithfulness or an immoral life-style—a continuous habit of promiscuity.

The suggestion is made that the injured mate may break the marriage relationship, but that it is not mandatory; the faithful partner may even learn to live with an unfaithful husband or wife and continue the marriage relationship. Or, if the unfaithful one repents and changes his or her life-style, then the faithful partner may forgive and the marriage may continue.

Another cause which some cite as justification for divorce is if one of the partners remains an unbeliever. The believing partner has a right to divorce according to some. In justification of this position one reads and quotes 1 Corinthians 7:12–15: "But to the rest speak I, not the Lord: If any brother hath a wife that believeth not, and she be pleased to dwell with him, let him not put her away. And the woman who hath a husband that believeth not, and if he be pleased to dwell with her, let her not leave him. For the unbelieving husband is sanctified by the wife, and the unbelieving wife is sanctified by the husband; else were your children unclean, but now are they holy. But if the unbelieving depart, let him depart. A brother or a sister is not under bondage in such cases; but God has called us to peace."

The Bible here is addressing the question of religiously-mixed marriage, when one or the other is not religiously committed. However, we should not assume that such marriages are always unhappy. We have all known cases where the wife or the husband accepted an unbelieving partner. We have seen certain married people come to church Sunday after Sunday alone and go home to a partner who never comes to church; yet seemingly they have a good and a happy marriage.

However, it does seem that the Bible gives the godly, committed person an "out" in that situation when it says, "A brother or a sister is not under bondage in such cases." We will not reach unanimity on the matter. In the final analysis, after studying, praying, and counsel, one has to make one's own decision.

Some time ago as I was studying our Lord's Sermon on the Mount, I set down what seems to me to be His teaching on divorce and remarriage. I later put those thoughts into my book, *The Sermon on the Mount.* The following is a quote of the biblical passage, Matthew 5:27–31, and my discussion of Jesus' words.

> Ye have heard that it was said by them of old time, Thou shalt not commit adultery:
>
> But I say unto you, That whosoever looketh on a woman to lust after her hath committed adultery with her already in his heart.
>
> And if thy right eye offend thee, pluck it out, and cast it from thee: for it is profitable for thee that one of thy members should perish, and not that thy whole body should be cast into hell.
>
> And if thy right hand offend thee, cut it off, and cast

it from thee: for it is profitable for thee that one of thy
members should perish, and not that thy whole body
should be cast into hell.

It hath been said, Whosoever shall put away his
wife, let him give her a writing of divorcement:

But I say unto you, That whosoever shall put away
his wife, saving for the cause of fornication, causeth
her to commit adultery: and whosover shall marry her
that is divorced committeth adultery.

(Matthew 5:27–32)

Just as Jesus went beyond murder to anger, now He goes beyond adultery to lust; then He proclaims the fact that it is not the
action but the attitude—the inner thought—that counts the
most. The thing we must keep in mind is: sin is a matter of one's
mind and heart. Our actions are merely the expressions of our
inward sin. And, of course, we all realize that our Lord was not
condemning the normal human desires which God put into people. What He was condemning was the deliberate intention to
lust. You remember it was Martin Luther who said, "We cannot
keep the birds from flying over our heads, but we can keep them
from building a nest in our hair."

To emphasize the importance of our inner thoughts, our Lord
uses very drastic illustrations, and talks about "plucking out" the
eye that offends us or "cutting off" our right hand when it offends. Of course, the words are not to be taken literally. If I were
to cut out my tongue, it would keep me from saying wrong
things, but on the other hand it would destroy my ability to say
kind and helpful things. If I pluck out my eye, it would keep me
from seeing the dirty and the suggestive, but also it would keep
me from seeing the beautiful and the true. If I cut off my hand, it
would keep me from hitting someone in anger, but it would also
prevent me from extending it in a firm handclasp of friendship.

In this passage, our Lord is emphasizing the fact that we must
deal sternly with our inner desires and feelings, and hold them in
complete check. And how is this to be done? By saying to ourselves, "We will not think about this"? The victory cannot be

gained in that way. For thirty-five years, St. Anthony lived the life of a hermit, struggling with his temptations. One night the devil took upon him the shape of a woman and imitated all of her acts before him. St. Anthony never did reach the point where he could overcome that.

Let me quote a passage from the writings of Dr. Clovis Chappell, which shows a better way: "The little schoolhouse that I attended years ago was surrounded by a great grove of scrubby black oak. These trees had a wonderful way of clinging to their leaves. When the frost killed other leaves and cut them from the boughs of the trees, these oak leaves still clung, though they were as dead as any that lay on the ground. Then came the sharp winds of winter. But, even they were powerless to break the hold of these dead leaves. Still later came the snow and the sleet and the ice, but their efforts were equally futile. But one day a wonderful surgeon clipped all those leaves away. Who was that surgeon? His name was Spring. Springtime got into the heart of those oaks and the sap rose up and the new leaves pushed out and said to the old dead leaves: 'This is my place.' And thus Christ will save us. Therefore, this I say, 'Walk in the spirit and you shall not fulfil the lust of the flesh.' "

Dr. Thomas Chalmers, the great Scot preacher, used to talk about "the expulsive power of a new affection."

Now, we come to one of the statements of our Lord that has caused untold concern in the hearts of many people. It brings up the whole matter of divorce. Is divorce ever permissible? If one has been divorced, and then marries again, is he living in sin?

Jesus said, *I say unto you, That whosoever shall put away his wife, saving for the cause of fornication, causeth her to commit adultery: and whosoever shall marry her that is divorced committeth adultery.* These words were laid down in a very definite day in which definite situations existed. In that day a woman had no rights; in the sight of the law she was merely a thing. Her husband had absolute power over her, and with just a word he could divorce her; there was no court that would protect her. Jesus would have the people know that marriage is the most sacred of all relations in life, and something not to be taken lightly

at all. However, the situation to which He addressed these words
has undergone a great change.

A bright and attractive young man came into my office; he
was obviously very worried. He and his wife had been very hap-
pily married for some five years. One day he read the words of
Christ in reference to the marriage of a divorced person. When
his wife was twenty years old, she had married another man; they
lived together for about a year, and then he deserted her. He
simply told her he was through and left. He gave her no support
and no help in any way. After waiting almost another year, all
the time being willing to take him back and try again, and hoping
he would return, the woman finally decided that her marriage
was over. So she went to court and got a divorce on the grounds
of desertion. Sometime after that, she and the young man who
came to see me met each other, and after a time, they fell in love
and were married. Their marriage had been extremely good until
he read the statement and became worried over it. He wanted to
know if he should immediately divorce his wife, even though he
loved her dearly. He felt that, in the light of Jesus' statement, he
and his wife had no right to be married.

I happen to be a minister in the Methodist Church, and so I
read to him the paragraph in the *Methodist Discipline*, which is
our book of law, referring to the marriage of divorced persons.
The paragraph reads thus: "In view of the seriousness with
which the Scriptures and the Church regard divorce, a minister
may solemnize the marriage of a divorced person only when he
has satisfied himself by careful counseling that: (a) the divorced
person is sufficiently aware of the factors leading to the failure of
the previous marriage, (b) the divorced person is sincerely pre-
paring to make the proposed marriage truly Christian, and (c)
sufficient time has elapsed for adequate preparation and counsel-
ling" (1964 edition, paragraph 356).

This did not satisfy him. He felt that no church had a right to
make any statement or rule in violation of the Bible. I agreed
with him fully at that point, but insisted that this was not in violation of Christ's Word. "How can that be," he said, "when the
matter is stated so plainly?"

I said to him, "I cannot show you any specific reference, but I can show you something better than that, and that is the Spirit of our Christ." I turned and read to him the story of the Prodigal Son, and talked about the love of a godly father who would forgive his sinful son and restore him to the home. I turned to the eighth chapter of the Gospel According to St. John, and read to him the story of a woman who was about to be stoned to death because of the sin of adultery. Together we saw how Christ dealt with her. After her accusers were gone, gently He said to her, "Neither do I condemn thee: go, and sin no more." He was saying to her, as the father of the prodigal was saying to him, "I am willing to give you another chance."

I talked to this young man about how, over and over, Jesus spoke of the fact that He came to save sinners, that He was the "Christ of Another Chance." "Now," I asked the young husband, "do you believe that Jesus would say to your wife: 'You married when you were twenty years old, and your marriage broke up. Whether it was your fault or not is beside the point. The point is that since you've been married once, you cannot be rightfully married again. If you do ever marry again, you and the man you marry will be living in sin. I forever forbid you the opportunity of another marriage, of a home, of children. You must live the remainder of your life alone.' "

We talked about it together, and we both agreed that such would not be the attitude of the Christ we knew in the Gospels. Surely, Jesus would have said to this young man's wife: "You made a mistake, but now you are sincere in wanting another chance, and I gladly give it to you."

As one minister, I cannot see any other position than the fact that even if one has failed in a marriage, if that one is sincere, and in the right spirit enters into another marriage, that marriage will have the blessing of God. I cannot feel that if one steals or lies, or even commits murder, God will forgive him, but the same God will never forgive one who has made a mistake in his or her marriage. I used to think that the words in the ceremony, "till death us do part," referred to the death of the physical body; but, across the years, after counseling with many, many people, I've come to realize that some other things can die, too. Respect can die. Love can die. Hope can die. And a marriage can die. Realizing this fact, it behooves every married couple to give their very best in keeping their marriage alive. But, sometimes, even the best efforts of one or both have failed, and the law of our land provides a way out. I do not feel that such unhappy people are beyond God's mercy.

Having said this, though, let us reemphasize the fact that marriage is the most important relationship in one's life, and when that relationship is broken, it leaves deep scars on the person. The saddest words the Lord ever spoke were these: "The foxes have holes, and the birds of the air have nests; but the Son of man hath not where to lay his head" (Matthew 8:20). One of the heaviest burdens He bore was the fact that He did not have a home. Through the years I have tried to help many couples persevere in their marriage, and many of them have succeeded. Edgar A. Guest was certainly right when he said, "It takes a heap o' livin' in a house t' make it home."

When two people marry, they should be in love; that first romantic love is a thrilling and beautiful experience. Marriage means that two people have given themselves to each other, and decided to go the same way together. In her book *Glimpses of the Moon*, Edith Wharton has one of the characters saying: "The point is that we are married . . . married. Doesn't that mean something to you, something—inexorable? It does to me. I didn't dream it would—in just that way. But all I can say is that I suppose the people who don't feel it aren't really married."

Marriage, however, is based on more than just that "inexorable" feeling. It must be a growing experience in which two people:

> . . . *share each other's woes,*
> *Each other's burdens bear,*
> *And often for each other flows*
> *The sympathizing tear.*

That first romantic love is nothing compared with the strength of the love that grows as two people walk down life's path together.

Ten

Forget Past Failures— Success Lies Ahead

In one sense people never really forget anything. Often some incident or experience that happened many, many years earlier will flash into one's mind; somehow the mind has a way of calling it to our conscious thinking. But for the most part, we can "forget" to the point that we are not bound by our past experiences.

Through the years I have counseled privately with many, many people and I am convinced that many are unsuccessful and unhappy and are living a seemingly condemned life because they have never learned how to forget. We carry in our minds the accumulation of our failures and past mistakes and this becomes a heavy burden that takes the joy out of living. Being bound by mistakes and the unhappiness of yesterday greatly reduces our capacity to live a meaningful and constructive life. And in extreme cases, this inability to forget produces mental sickness that is far more serious than any spiritual sickness.

Two men met in the street one afternoon downtown. They were old friends but had not seen each other in many, many years. At first they sat down in the lobby of a hotel and began to talk about old times. Then they decided to go into the dining room and eat dinner together. After dinner they continued talking and enjoyed reliving the past so much that before they realized it, it was three o'clock in the morning. They had been so engrossed in each other that they had forgotten to call home. They both went home a little fearful of what their wives would say about their being so late.

The next day they met again and one said, "What did your wife say about your coming in at three o'clock in the morning?" His friend replied, "Oh, I explained it to her and it was perfectly all right. What did your wife say?"

The man replied, "Oh, when I came in she got historical."

"You mean hysterical," came the rely.

"No, I mean historical. She brought up everything that had happened the past thirty years."

None of us want to lose our memories but sometimes it is good to forget in the sense that we quit bringing it up. One of the wisest psychologists America has ever known was William James. He once said, "The most important factor in the art of being wise is the art of knowing what to overlook." That is a profound observation. If you want to be wise, learn how to overlook some things. Know what you should wipe out—put aside—quit purposely remembering.

Turn to the third chapter of St. Paul's letter to the Philippians and read the thirteenth verse. It says, "Brethren, I count not myself to have apprehended; but this one thing I do, forgetting those things which are behind, and reaching forth unto those things which are before. . . ."

Truly, a good memory is a great asset. There is a story to the effect that the great Larry George on one occasion was walking through a pasture gate with a friend. He noticed that the friend did not shut the gate, so turned around, went back and locked it.

"Never walk through a gate that you do not turn around and shut," he said to his friend. And one of the essentials of a successful life is to be able to walk through an issue and then shut the gate and keep walking. Life is full of "ends," but for every end there is always a beginning. Underscore that word *always*. There is no such thing as an end, period. Even death is not an end, period. Every night has a morning.

Through the years I have enjoyed moving streams, rivers, and even tiny brooks. A moving stream is constantly going somewhere. The old Greek Heraclitus said: "You can't step in the same river twice." In a very real sense life is like a river. The river begins up in the heights as a very small tiny stream. It journeys down through the hills. The river steadily continues its journey onward and the fact that it moves continually indicates it is filled with life-giving waters.

Life is like a river. We start out little but we keep moving and we pick up new experiences, new insights, new knowledge—but we keep moving. Once we stop we become stagnated. Creative work and dreams of where we are going means growth and freshness.

We know that love is the deepest of all emotions. We read that St. Paul said, "And now abideth faith, hope, love, these three; but the greatest of these is love" (1 Corinthians 13:13). There is no greater experience on this earth than love. Love is the most powerful force humanity has ever known. When a marriage began in love and is lived in love, and when that love is gone, it is a traumatic experience, an experience that one never forgets—an experience one never "gets over." But in the sense that it does not freeze a life, one does in a very real sense "forget" and go on.

Eleven

Our Disappointment—
God's Appointment _____

Disappointment is one of life's experiences that we never get away from. Disappointment happens over and over regardless of one's age or circumstances.

I still remember when I was in the third grade at school and we were planning for our class Christmas tree. Some of us went out into the woods and got a tree and brought it in to decorate it. We were so proud of that tree, and as we thought about Christmas we became more and more excited. We drew names to see who would bring a present to whom. All of us brought our presents on the last morning of school before the holidays and placed them under the tree until the close of that school day when they would all be passed out. None of us were really interested in what was going on that day in school. We were looking and wondering which one of those presents might be ours and what it would be.

Finally the time came for our Christmas celebration. The teacher led us in some Christmas carols and told us the Christmas story; then came the high moment when the presents would be passed out. The teacher picked up a present, called a name and that student walked forward and proudly claimed his present. Then she picked up another present and called another name. I remember sitting there, a little boy eagerly anticipating my name being called. Finally the last present was given out and my name had never been called. The one who had drawn my name was sick and was not at school that day. Therefore I had no present. As long as I live I will remember the disappointment of being at the Christmas party and my name never being called. That to me was disappointment.

We have all experienced disappointments of various kinds. A boy in a little town one night slipped under the side of a big tent. He thought the circus had come to town, but after he got in he found out that he was in a revival meeting. You can imagine his letdown.

There is a poem which says:

> Thou art indeed just, Lord, if I contend
> with thee; so what I plead is just.
> Why do sinners' ways prosper? And why must
> Disappointment all I endeavor end?
> *Rod Evan Hopkins*

Many of us can identify with the feeling of that poem. However, I doubt if many disappointments are greater than that which divorce brings. Most marriages are entered into in a spirit of high hope, and when a marriage is dissolved, usually somebody is deeply hurt and deeply disappointed.

Actually, disappointment spares no person and no life, but the quality of life is in how one handles disappointment. Many times, even though God does not cause the disappointment, that disappointment can turn out to be one of God's appointments. I am not suggesting that divorce is ever God's appointment; but as one moves out into life beyond divorce, that disappointed person often finds something great and good and worthwhile to live for. There are many, many illustrations of this fact.

Consider the experience of the great apostle St. Paul. In reference to him, the Bible records these words: "After they were come to Mysia, they assayed to go into Bithynia; but the Spirit suffered them not. And they, passing by Mysia, came down to Troas" (Acts 16:7, 8).

St. Paul dreamed of going into Bithynia, the wealthiest and most cultured province of Asia. Carrying the Christian message there was for him the crowning opportunity. But circumstances blocked his path. We are not sure why he could not enter Bithynia, but we do know he landed in Troas—a poor unpromising place. Surely he was disappointed.

However, instead of giving up he decided to work in Troas. He took advantage of whatever opportunities he could find there to proclaim his message and carry out his ministry. And in Troas he heard one saying, "Come over into Macedonia, and help us" (Acts 16:9). He did not realize it then, but now we know that that was the invitation to the largest service he was ever privileged to render. He went into Macedonia and in that action the Christian gospel was planted in Europe. From there it grew and flourished and went out unto the uttermost parts of the earth. There are those who believe that if Paul had gone to Bithynia, as he so badly wanted, we would never have heard of him today. Out of his great disappointment came his greatest opportunity. This has happened over and over.

Do you remember when you left home and went to college or went to work someplace and established your own home? That was not an easy experience. Sometimes we get the notion that permanence is a gift of God and of life and when change comes we have been singled out for punishment.

As I write these words, I am thinking of one of my children

who lives ten minutes away from me. It is truly a comforting joy when I think that I can run out and see these loved ones at any time. It also gives me a sense of security to know that if I were to become ill or needed anything I could pick up the telephone and in moments someone who loves me would be by my side. Recently my dear child told me that they may move to another state due to their business. Of course I want them to live where they are the best off and where they feel they should go. In fact, I am excited that they are entering into a position of greater opportunity and promise. But the change is somewhat sobering for me and also for them. It means that the children would be changing schools and leaving their friends, and leaving the home that they call good living.

Change is going to come no matter what. We may as well make up our minds about that.

Marriage is change, but it is change with great anticipation. Death is change, but it is change with sorrow. Divorce is change, and certainly it is a change also with sorrow and many times with great fear. When we think of death we think of God being responsible for that happening. When we think of divorce, we feel the burden upon ourselves and sometimes we wonder if even God is there to help us.

Whenever I go to Boston I like to visit Trinity Church of which Phillips Brooks was the minister. In front of that church is a statue of him. He is revered and respected. However, before Phillips Brooks became a minister, he had a dream of being a teacher. But as a teacher he failed. At one time he was so depressed he said, "I do not know what will ever become of me and I really do not much care." But later he became a minister, and a truly good one. A little girl once said of him, "When I get to heaven, I want to sit by Doctor Brooks." Maybe his disappointment was God's appointment.

We think of Sir Walter Scott who has been called the "king of romantics." His greatest dream was to be a poet and he worked hard at it. But as a poet he failed. Finally he wrote a novel, but he would not let it be published under his name for he was ashamed of having failed as a poet. Later he wrote many other novels—

Waverley, Ivanhoe, and *Rob Roy* among them. As a novelist Sir Walter Scott achieved literary greatness—a greatness that came out of disappontment.

When the United States government wanted to issue a stamp honoring the mothers of America, the portrait they chose was the one that Whistler painted of his mother. It is one of the most revered and loved portraits in the world. If you view the life of Whistler you will find that he wanted to be a soldier in the United States Army. He went to West Point, but there he failed and had to leave school. Later he tried engineering and he failed there. As a last resort he took up painting. Out of his disappointment came his greatest accomplishment.

Thinking of paintings one is reminded of Jean François Millet, one of the greatest painters of all time. His works of art—*The Gleaning, The Angelus, Shepherds and Flock,* and *The Man With a Hoe*—are great and deeply appreciated throughout the world. His first painting to be accepted was one entitled *Oedipus Unbound.* But that was not Millet's first painting. He painted a portrait entitled Saint Jerome, which was completely rejected. No one would accept it. Millet was so poor he could not afford to buy another canvas for another picture, so he took this rejected portrait and began to paint over it; this became *Oedipus Unbound.* His success came on top of his disappointment.

Nobody ever promised that life would be easy and pleasant all the way. At no time have we ever been promised that all our dreams would come true. One of the most read and beloved authors America has ever produced is Lloyd C. Douglas. He wrote *Magnificent Obsession, Forgive Us Our Trespasses, Green Light, The Robe,* and many other books. However, Lloyd C. Douglas wanted to be a physician, but that door was closed to him. He had to give up what he most wanted, but out of his disappointment came great victories and great accomplishments.

One of the dreams of King David in the Bible was to build a temple. He even gathered a great many of the materials for the temple, but he never got to build it. His son Solomon built the temple, and David never saw it. Undoubtedly David died with a deep disappointment. The temple was to be his crowning accom-

plishment. However, today the temple is gone, but the Twenty-
third Psalm, which he wrote, continues to bless the lives of mul-
tiplied millions of people. I doubt if David thought he had
accomplished much with that short little psalm, but he accomplished more than he would have accomplished by building a
temple.

As a minister one of the great joys I have is lecturing to
groups of tourists in the Holy Land. One can take tours to many
places, but going to Israel is not a tour—it is an experience. It is
always very moving to stand and look at the hill where many believe is the place Jesus was crucified. As we stand there we think
about His dreams and hopes of the kingdom of God on earth; instead, He ended on a cross. But as someone has written:

> *All the light of sacred story*
> *Gathers 'round its head sublime.*

I am taking some time at this point because I think it is so important. We do not believe that God sends disappointment, but
we do believe that disappointments are inevitable as we move
through life. Disappointment can cut deeply and hurt terribly.
Disappointment can be a wound to the soul and, like a wound to
the physical body, can become infected. So might disappointment
become an infected wound in our soul. Out of disappointment
can come anger, hate, jealousy, worry, a feeling of unworthiness,
a feeling of failure, discouragement, hopelessness, and more and
more infection.

A friend of mine slipped and fell not long ago and broke his
wrist. When the doctor removed the cast, the man's wrist was
still swollen and painful. He asked the doctor how much longer it
would be until the pain was gone and the doctor told him that his
wrist would never be as it was. It would always be somewhat re-
stricted and there would always be some pain connected with it.
In commenting upon it my friend said, "I made one slip and I
have to suffer for it the rest of my life."

That is what we feel many times about divorce. However, divorce is not the end. It is a new beginning.

One of America's greatest writers was Thomas Carlyle. He once suffered a disappointment that could have destroyed his career. He set out to write a most serious and difficult book. It took him four years of hard labor to get his notes in shape and after that he set in to write the book. As he would finish a section, he would feel such joy that he would throw away his old notes. Finally, after six years the book was finished and he took the manuscript to his dear friend John Stuart Mill and asked him to read it. It took Mill five days to read it and he realized what a marvelous work it was, one of the classics of literary history. When he finished reading it he left it on the floor, planning to take it the next morning to his friend. Early that morning the maid came in to make the fire in the sitting room. Seeing these papers on the floor, she thought they were trash that Mill was throwing away and so she picked them up and threw them into the fire. When Mill realized what had happened, he went with agony and deep sorrow to tell his friend that his work of six years had been destroyed. With a smile, Carlyle said, "It's all right. I will start over again in the morning."

Carlyle watched Mill from the window as he walked back across the field toward his home, and then he turned to his wife and said, "Poor Mill, I feel so sorry for him. I did not want him to see how crushed I really am." Then he said, "Well, I had better start writing again."

Divorce can be crushing, but there comes a time when we "had better start writing again."

Twelve

Burn Your Past— Fix Your Future _____

One of the most meaningful services I ever conducted as the minister of a church was the Sunday night service just preceding New Year's Eve. I used this plan a number of times. As the people entered the church for the service, each one received a slip of paper, and as the service began I explained to them its purpose. One side was for dealing with the past and the other was for dealing with the future. I further explained that the paper was small for a very good reason. I wanted everybody to be very specific as they used that slip of paper.

Through the years, I have enjoyed hunting birds, especially quail. However, for a long time I was not a very good shot. Then one day a man told me why I killed so few birds. He explained that when a covey of quail rose up, I would shoot at all of them at once. He told me that when anyone shoots at the covey he rarely ever hits any. Instead, he told me that no matter how many quail there are, I should pick out one bird, get it clearly in my sights, and then pull the trigger. After he explained that to me, I began to practice what he had told me and I became a much better shot and brought home a lot more birds.

There is one of the problems with praying. So many times we ask God to forgive our sins, our past mistakes, or our failures. There is not really very much power in that kind of prayer. There is marvelous wisdom in the Bible verse which says, "Wherefore, seeing we also are compassed about with so great a cloud of witnesses, let us lay aside every weight, and the sin which doth so easily beset us, and let us run with patience the race that is set before us" (Hebrews 12:1). Notice, it does not say "Let us lay aside . . . all our past sins." Instead it says, "the sin." There is marvelous power when we get specific. We can talk about past mistakes and failures, but when we fix our mind on a definite failure, then we have some place to start and something to work on. So first, I tell the people to decide on one specific thing that they want to overcome, to get forgiveness for, to put behind them as they enter a new year.

As we pray the Lord's Prayer we say, "Forgive us our trespasses, as we forgive those who have trespassed against us." In my special New Year's service I suggest to people that instead of saying "trespasses" they use the singular and pick out one trespass. Then I suggest instead of saying, "we forgive *those* who have trespassed against us," that we substitute for "those" a specific name. Think of one person, I tell them; name that person and forgive that one person.

Not long ago someone asked me, "Will God hear my prayers if I have done wrong?"

I quoted to that person these words: "If I regard iniquity in

my heart, the Lord will not hear me" (Psalms 66:18). Then I
asked him: "What have you done wrong?"

He replied, "Lots of things."

"You did not come to me because you were bothered about
lots of things," I said. "You came because you were bothered
about a certain specific thing."

On that Sunday night before New Year's I urge every person
to write down one special something—a transgression, a worry, a
disappointment, a hurt, a bad decision, a person to forgive—
something he or she wants to leave in the old year and get rid of.

It helps to write it down. Not only are we more specific but it
fixes it in our mind.

Then I say to the people that I want them to completely decide then and there if they want to put what they have written
down out of their life forever. Actually the mind is divided into
parts—there is the part we think with, and another part we feel
with. Just to think about something we would like to settle is not
enough. We must feel it and really want to do it.

I have a stupid little story from which I always get a laugh. At
a scout meeting one night the scoutmaster asked the boys what
good turn they had done that day. One little boy held up his hand
and said, "I helped an old lady across the street." The second little boy held up his hand and said, "I helped the same old lady
across the street." Then a third little boy held up his hand and
said, "I helped the same old lady across the street."

The scoutmaster said, "Why did it take all three of you to
help the same old lady across the street?"

One of the little scouts replied, "The old lady didn't want to
go across the street."

Right at this point is the problem a lot of us face—we really do
not want to settle this thing that is worrying us. Georgia Hark-
ness had a way of saying, "Be careful what you set your heart on,
for you will surely get it."

One of the precious promises of the Bible is this one: "If we
confess our sins, he is faithful and just to forgive us our sins, and
to cleanse us from all unrighteousness" (1 John 1:9). But con-

fession is more than just admitting something. Confession is also feeling something. And when we begin to confess with our minds and our feelings, marvelous things are going to happen.

Not only must we decide exactly what it is that needs to be settled. Not only must we decide that we want it settled. We need to decide that we want it settled now. That word *now* is a powerful word. Turn those three little letters n-o-w around and you end up with the word w-o-n, *won*. The reason we are defeated so many times is we are always saying that someday we want to deal with this thing.

I have another story that I have enjoyed through the years. One day a man walked into a bus station and bought a ticket for Smithville. While he was waiting for the bus he saw a machine over in the corner with a sign on it saying that it would tell one's fortune. So he decided he would try it. He went over, put a dime in the machine, and pulled the handle. The machine spun around and said, "Your name is John Doe, you weigh a hundred and fifty pounds, and you are fixing to catch the bus to Smithville."

He was literally amazed. He looked all around the machine and studied it and kept wondering how that machine could know that about him. After a while he decided he would try it again, so he put in his dime. The machine spun around again and said, "Your name is John Doe, you weigh a hundred and fifty pounds, and you are fixing to catch the bus to Smithville." Once more he was amazed. He stood and studied it and then tried it again. Then after a while, again. Finally, he had one dime left. "I'm going to try it one more time," he said. So he put his dime in, the machine spun around and it said, "Your name is John Doe, you weigh a hundred and fifty pounds, and you have fooled around so long you have missed the bus."

If you think that story is stupid, wait a minute. I have one that is worse than that. . . .

These three turtles went into a drugstore to get a Coca-Cola. After the man had fixed the Coca-Colas they realized they had left their money at home. So they drew straws to see who would go home and get the money. Charlie Turtle lost and he said, "I'll go and get the money if you will promise me you will not drink the Coca-Colas until I come back." They promised and so he started out the door.

As we all know, turtles are slow and Charlie Turtle was especially slow. The other two turtles waited a week, and he hadn't come back. Then a month, and then three months, and still he hadn't come back. By that time they were getting a little thirsty and the Coca-Colas which had been poured into the glasses were getting a little warm so they decided they would just take a sip of the Coca-Colas. When they reached up to get their glasses, Charlie Turtle stuck his head in the door and said, "Now watch out boys. If you drink them I won't go."

There is a point to these stories. If we are going to do something we must decide now is the time to do it.

In my service I would stop here and have the people write down on the slip of paper what they are going to write. I would reemphasize again and again: be definite—want to settle it—want to settle it *now*.

After I had given everybody time to do their writing I would say one other thing—"Trust in the power of God to help you." None of us is strong enough, but God is strong enough. Then I would quote two verses from the Bible—"My God shall supply all your need according to his riches in glory by Christ Jesus" (Philippians 4:19). And: "If my people, which are called by my name, shall humble themselves, and pray, and seek my face, and turn from their wicked ways; then will I hear from heaven, and will forgive their sin, and will heal their land" (2 Chronicles 7:14).

I would keep saying to the people that God will help them and that God has promised that if we will do our part He will do His part. Our part is to recognize our inabililty to heal ourselves, to ask God's help and to turn away from that thing in our lives that we want to leave to the past. God's part is to hear what we say, to forgive and bring healing to our hearts and our souls and our bodies.

Really and truly, that is about the best swap any one of us could make. Can you imagine a better bargain? Really there is

great joy and power over feeling that a debt has been settled—
sin has been forgiven—a mistake has been left in the past.

One of the characters in *Hans Frost* by Hugh Walpole speaks
of certain people who "slap the face of the present with the dead
hand of the past." It is a glorious thing when a past sin has been
left behind—when a past mistake has been left behind—when
the past literally is the past. That does not mean that we completely forget yesterday. The truth is we never forget anything.
But it does mean that we stop slapping our face with yesterday.

Next I say to the people, "Turn that slip of paper over. You
notice it is blank. The other side represents the future. Now I
want you to write down one resolution." There is not room there
for a long dissertation so I take them through the same process
which I repeat over and over—be definite—really want to do
it—start right now—trust God's help. Those same four principles apply in reference to our resolution.

Oftentimes we say, "I have thought about doing that," or "I
intend sometime to do that," or "I have planned on doing that."
But there comes a time when we say, "This is the night." New
Year's Eve is a night to dream. I know some people laugh at
dreamers but I say that no person ever rises higher or goes further than his dreams.

I know a man who achieved outstanding success as a business
leader in America. In talking about his life, he told of growing up
on a farm in the mountains of Tennessee. Near where he lived
was a railroad track and twice a day a passenger train came thun-
dering along that track. He used to go outside and look at the
train as it went by. He could see the people in the train. Some
were sitting in pullman cars, some were sitting on the observation platform, some were in the dining car, eating. He would
dream that someday he too would ride on that train. After that
train had gone out of sight, he would hear a whistle far in the
distance and he felt like it was a call to him to do something and
be something. Later in life he said that nothing was more responsible for the accomplishments which were his than seeing
that train and hearing that whistle and dreaming of someday
being one of those people.

And so I talk with the people about putting down one dream—one goal—one ambition—one hope.

Many times I have quoted to myself those enthusiastic lines from "Rabbi Ben Ezra" by Robert Browning:

> *The best is yet to be, the last of life,*
> *for which the first was made. . . .*

The Chinese word for *tomorrow* is composed of two words, "bright day."

Sometime ago I heard about someone who had a very hard, difficult life. When asked how he could stand to keep on living, he said, "The things that saved me are my 'gonnas.' When I got sick I would say, 'I'm gonna get well.' When my team lost the ball game I would say, 'They are gonna win tomorrow.' When I would feel blue or discouraged I would say, 'I am gonna feel better tomorrow.' " He pointed out that no matter what happened or how bad the situation might be, he could always come up with some "gonnas." Those were the things that kept him going and kept him excited.

It is a great thing to decide on some one specific resolution and then, in that church service on Sunday night before New Year's, after the people had written on both sides of the paper, I would give them the opportunity to come to the altar and kneel. After they had prayed the prayer that was in their hearts they would put that slip of paper in a container behind the altar in which candles were burning. They would watch it burn up, and then would walk out free and determined—shackles were removed and inspiration for living was gained.

Countless numbers of people saw their lives completely changed in that experience.

I have gone to some length about that Sunday night church service. Now I want to suggest to the reader of this book that you reread what I have said about this service and go through it step by step yourself. Really do it. Then when it's all finished, let that slip of paper burn up and your life can be new and different and great.

The experience of divorce can be likened unto the New Year; it contains both the past and the future. The future represents a new chance and a new opportunity. I urge the reader of these pages to use that slip of paper.

Thinking of yesterday and of tomorrow and of the New Year, some lines from a song keep coming to my mind. It's "Let's Start the New Year Right" which Bing Crosby sang in the motion picture, *Holiday Inn*. The lines I remember go like this:

> *One minute to midnight,*
> *One minute to go;*
> *One minute to say goodbye,*
> *Before we say hello.*

Thirteen

How to Maintain
a Calm Confidence
in Tomorrow

On my desk is a letter which says, "Please tell me how to re-gain confidence in tomorrow and to face the future with calm-ness. I realize I can't do much about the past. I can work with the present; but when I think of all that might happen in the fu-ture, I feel helpless and afraid."

This is a normal concern for any person, but especially for those who have had some traumatic experience in their lives. Di-vorce is certainly one of the most traumatic. As someone has put it: "Divorce is when it all comes tumbling down." Marriage is a

time of exciting and new beginnings. For many, divorce is a time
of a very uncertain and sometimes even a very fearful tomorrow.
In answer to that request by mail, and in answer to those who are
seeking a calm confidence in tomorrow I try to say three things:

First, believe that life is good. The Bible says, "And we know
that all things work together for good to them that love God"
(Romans 8:28). The truth of the matter is that not everybody
"knows" that. Many, many people feel that things work together
for bad.

We need to remember that the Bible does not say that everything that happens is good. Life is composed of both joy and sorrow, of both victory and defeat, of both success and failure. We
know that tomorrow will most likely bring forth both good and
bad in our lives. The important thing to think about and to remember is that the Bible does not say everything that happens is
good, but "all things work together for good."

Let me illustrate. Think of a ship. The purpose of a ship is to
sail across the seas, but not all parts of a ship will float upon the
water. For example, the engine, if put on the water, would immediately sink. So would the propeller, the compass, and many
other parts of the ship. But when all of the parts of the ship are
securely built together, then it will sail across even the roughest
seas.

So it is with life. Some things that happen to people are bad.
Some things are good. But when we consider all the experiences
of life, using our love for God as the cement that holds all of life's
experiences together, then, taken as a whole, life works out for
good. We do not ask for the assurance that all the sorrow and
disappointment and troubles and hurts will be eliminated from
our tomorrows. We do not ask to be put in some isolated area
where nothing bad can ever happen to us. That is not good.

Some time ago a father came to visit with me. He was bro-
kenhearted. His son, a student in college, had been at home for
the weekend and while driving back to school he had had an accident and was killed. The father kept saying over and over to me,
"If I had not given him that car, he would never have been
killed." I tried to talk with the father and say that this is one of

the chances of life. He could have kept that boy in the house and never let him go outside and the boy would never have had that wreck and would never have been killed. But on the other hand his life would have been wrecked and it might have been an even greater tragedy. If we expect to go somewhere, we are compelled to take some chances. If we are protected from all of the chances of hurt then we are shut off from all of the chances of joy.

A Greek legend tells about a woman who came to the River Styx to be carried across to the next life. Charon, the man who ran the ferry, reminded her that she could drink the waters of Lethe and thus forget the life she was leaving. Eagerly she said, "I will forget how I have suffered." But he pointed out, "You will also forget how you have rejoiced."

"I will forget my failures," she said. "And you will forget your victories," he added.

"I will forget how I have been hated," she said. "And also you will forget how you have been loved."

The story ends with her deciding that it is better to retain her memories of the bad in order to also retain her memory of the good.

So it is with tomorrow. If by drinking some magic water we could eliminate all the suffering, the failure, and the hate of tomorrow, would we eagerly do it? Especially when we remember that life is always two-sided, and to destroy one side necessarily destroys the other. In eliminating the bad we would also eliminate the joys, the victories, and the love. Hardly any of us would be willing to drink the magic water. We would rather say, "Give us both the good and the bad."

Some things that happen in life are bad. Some things that happen are good. But life itself can be trusted, and if we would consider it all as one whole and not just pick out specific experiences, then we can say with St. Paul, "We know that all things work together for good to them that love God." That is, no matter what happens we will keep on loving God and being faithful to life; we will face tomorrow with hope instead of fear, and when all of the pieces of life are put together we will see it has been good.

Why do we worry about tomorrow? Not because we are afraid something bad might happen. We know that sorrows and defeats lie ahead for us. We know this because we have already experienced sorrows and defeats and we know that there is a sameness about both yesterday and tomorrow.

Ever so often someone asks me, "What excites you the most about being in the Holy Land?" I cannot pick out any one place or one experience. It is all so thrilling to me and each day there is more exciting than the next.

However, one experience really stands out in my mind. One day I was talking with a dear friend there, a man about seventy years old, and something came up about the Twenty-third Psalm. As we talked he said to me, "Would you like to visit The Valley of the Shadow of Death?"

I replied that I was familiar with that term from the Twenty-third Psalm, but that I could not imagine there is such a place.

He explained to me that it does literally exist. It is between Bethlehem and Jericho, he said—Bethlehem being among the places with the highest elevation in all Israel, Jericho being the lowest in elevation of any city in the world. In the fall of the year when the colder weather set in and the grass had died, shepherds used to take their sheep down to Jericho to graze for a month or so. On the way, they would pass through this valley. On the sides of the valley were caves where wild animals made their homes. Also in the valley were small bands of robbers who would lie in wait for the shepherds and rob them as they came through. It was a very dangerous place and therefore had been named, "The Valley of the Shadow of Death."

When he explained to me that it really exists and that we could go and see it I was truly excited. The next morning he came to pick me up at the hotel. He drove a very small car, explaining that the roads were so rough that a larger car could not get there. On the way we had to get out several times and push the car over very rough and difficult places. Finally we stopped.

"There it is," he said, pointing ahead of us. I think I have never had such a thrill in my life as I did in seeing that sight that day. We walked down into the valley and spent the next several hours there. I saw the running water and could imagine a little sheep falling into that running water and becoming injured or even drowning. Then I saw tiny little ponds of water along the way and I thought of how the shepherd led the sheep "beside the still waters." There the little sheep could drink without fear.

I saw the little plots of grass along the way and I thought about the words, "He maketh me to lie down in green pastures."

The thing that thrilled me the most was that as we walked down that valley I kept thinking about those words: "Yea, though I walk through the valley of the shadow of death, I will fear no evil: for thou art with me."

As I think about that experience I keep underscoring in my own mind that word *through*. Somehow, since that day I have had more confidence and less fear of the future. We can stand most anything—defeat—pain—disappointment—sorrow—loss—and on and on—if we know we are going to get through. No defeat ever needs to be final. Somehow defeat works out for good.

Second, our fears of tomorrow can be overcome when we look forward with hope. One of the purest gems of all literature is *In Memoriam.* In it we find this wonderful line, "The mighty hopes that make us men." Hope gives strength to life. On the other hand, "Hope deferred maketh the heart sick" (Proverbs 13:12).

Someone recently made a study of a large group of people working in a certain company. They all did similar kinds of tasks yet, at the close of the day some were limp with fatigue while others seemed strong and rested. It was discovered that one group had something to look forward to—a party that night, a weekend trip, something ahead that was good. The other group had nothing to look forward to and all they were thinking about was the difficulty of their work that day.

Hope not only lifts our spirits; it gives vitality to our physical bodies. Something definite and specific to hope for is very important. Hope is never real until it becomes definite.

Two questions that so-called "hopeless" people need to ask

and answer are: 1) What is something I really want in life? (Of course, it is good to think of great goals, but it is also good to think of something close at hand. It does not have to be big and earthshaking; it can be very small. Even hoping for something small can be good.) 2) How can I get started toward the attainment of what I am hoping for?

Many times we discover that we can begin right now. Often people tell me of their plans and dreams of writing a book and I invariably ask when they intend to write it. Usually the answer is some vague, indefinite time. My suggestion is, "Go home tonight and write one page." After a person has written that first page, the rest of the pages are not nearly so difficult. Getting started is what's important.

As we think about tomorrow, the *third* thing to always remember is that we need resources beyond our own strengths. No one of us is wise enough, strong enough, or good enough. The word *pray* means different things to different people. But whatever you think about prayer, always remember that the words *praying* and *hoping* are completely compatible. Over and over I think of those words of the psalmist: "Why art thou cast down, O my soul? and why art thou disquieted within me? hope thou in God . . ." (Psalms 42:11). God and hope go together and we can say again and again—God has never broken any promise ever spoken.

Whatever You Ask For

One of the most thrilling promises ever made on this earth are the words of Jesus: "And whatsoever ye shall ask in my name, that will I do . . ." (John 14:13). However, in reference to that glorious promise, we must remember four essential facts.

1. God has already put within our reach the "whatsoever." A schoolboy was facing a very difficult examination the next day. He prayed earnestly that God would

give him a good mark on his exam. However, after he had taken the exam and the teacher gave him his grade he learned that he had failed. He got an "F." He became very bitter, disillusioned and resentful. God had promised—he had prayed—but the promise did not turn out good. He had to repeat the course the next year.

When he took the course over he decided he did not need God, and that he would depend on himself. So day by day he studied diligently. When time came for the examination, he went over all of his notes, applied his mental capacity and prepared thoroughly. He passed the course with high marks.

It took that boy some years to realize that God had answered his prayer even before he had prayed it. God gave him the mental ability to learn and to study. God gave him the opportunity to go to school. The problem was, he had not used God's answer. Many times in our lives, God has already provided the abilities and the resources and the opportunities to make our "whatsoevers" come true.

2. God has both the wisdom and the love for each one of us to distinguish between what we really want and what we think we want at the moment. Oftentimes there is a great difference. Any one of us could look back in our lives and see times when we prayed for something that we did not get, and now we know we did not really want it.

When I was a little boy, living in Winterville, Georgia, I used to see the junk man who went all over the community gathering junk. He had a wagon and a horse. I made friends with him and one summer I rode with him many days. He would let me drive the horse and it was great fun. I would help him gather up the junk and oftentimes at the close of the day he would give me twenty-five cents. I felt like I was really making important money. When September came, I told my father that I did not want to go back to school. Instead I wanted to work with the junk man and when I grew up I would like to be a junk man on my own. At that time I could not think of anything more exciting than having my own horse and wagon and my own business.

Suppose my father had said, "All right. You have thought about it, you know what you want, I am going to grant your desire"? That would have been a great tragedy in my life. Being wiser and more understanding, my father could distinguish between my dreams of the moment and the real desires in my heart for the life ahead. He refused my request and did not do what I had asked him. But in the much larger sense, he made it possible for me to have the real desires of my heart.

Tagore once said, "Thou didst save me by *thy hard refusals.*" Very fortunately for each one of us, God hears all of our prayers, but he answers our larger prayers.

One of the greatest disappointments I ever experienced came later in my life. I had finished Young Harris Junior College in north Georgia. At that time my father was the pastor of some very small churches; it was during the Great Depression and my father's resources were limited. After I had finished junior college, he told me that it would be good for me to get a job and work a year or two and let my brother John, who had just finished high school, go to college. He felt there was no way he could send both of us.

Not far from where we lived was a rural school—it was called Chipley then but now the name is Pine Mountain— and I applied for a teaching position there. I had been assured by some of the trustees that I would be accepted, and so my hopes were high. But I felt great disappointment and despair when they announced that they had selected someone else. I did not know which way to turn. Then somebody told me about Wofford College in Spartanburg, South Carolina.

At that time I had never been outside of the state of Georgia. Spartanburg, South Carolina, was a long ways away to me. But I wrote to Doctor Henry Nelson Snyder, the president of Wofford College, to inquire if there were any way I could enroll there. Later, as I came to know Dr. Snyder, I realized he was a great man. Through the years I have come to feel that he was one of the greatest men I have ever known. He wrote me back and told me to come to Wofford College; they would help me and I could continue my schooling. I went and they did help me. I do not say it boastfully, but with deep gratitude; one of the most prized possessions of my life is a Phi Beta Kappa key that I received from Wofford College. From there I went on to the seminary and then into the ministry.

When I lost that opportunity to teach school, I really felt that God had not heard my prayers. But now as I look back, I realize that God opened doors I did not even know existed. And God answered prayers for me that at that time I did not even know how to pray.

Parents often can distinguish between what their children think they want and what they really want. We are all so glad that we have a heavenly parent who is God.

3. God is concerned with all of His children. I grew up in a home as one of seven children and as I have indicated, we had a great life but we were not the wealthiest people around. I have many memories of those early years and one of the memories is Mama cooking a pie. Carefully she would divide it into nine pieces—one piece for each of the children, one piece for Father, and one piece for her. I learned early that I could not rightfully ask for two pieces of pie because that would mean that if my request were granted, somebody would have no pie at all. As I make my requests known to God, I need to remember that I am part of a great family of humanity.

Through the years, I have spoken in many places all over this nation and other nations. Usually I have no problem making plane reservations. However, one time really stands out in my mind. I phoned the airline and was told that no reservations were available. So I told them to put me on the standby list. I went to the airport, confidently believing that when the time came there would be a place for me. I prayed God to grant my request for a seat on the airplane. Arriving at the airport I went to the desk and presented my ticket. The man said that he would have to wait and see if there was room, and that he would call my name. In time the plane was called and the passengers filed in. I kept waiting and waiting, but my name never was called. No place opened up and the ticket agent handed back my ticket. The plane took off without me.

As I thought about it I knew that God could have managed

to get somebody off that plane. However, my better judgment told me that that would not have been fair. I really did not get too upset about it. Instead, I immediately made a reservation on the next available plane.

In our families we like to feel that our parents love each one of the children. We remember when we went to school, we wanted to feel that the teachers were fair to all of the students. So it is in the larger realm; we know that we are a part of the human family and that other people have their rights too. We want the blessings of God, but we also want the blessings of God for all other people. We do not want God to bless us at the expense of someone else.

4. As we think about the future, we need to remember these lines from our national anthem:

> *Then conquer we must,*
> *when our cause it is just,*
> *And this be our motto:*
> *"In God is our trust."*

It may be, and it often is, that our "whatsoevers" are not just or right or fair or good.

To me, one of the most thrilling places on this earth is the Garden of Gethsemane. Every time I visit it, I stand there in utter awe. Olive trees like the ones under which Jesus prayed that night are there. Many times I have stood there and wondered just where is the place Jesus and His disciples stood. There in the Garden of Gethsemane He was facing a life-or-death decision. Jesus loved life and lived life in a glorious way. He had high and holy purposes and there was so much to be done. He prayed with His disciples. Then He moved a little further away with Peter, James, and John, His three best friends.

Oftentimes we become a little discouraged when we think that maybe we do not have many real close friends. The truth is, nobody has many real close friends. If you have three you are doing good. Peter, James, and John were Jesus' three closest friends and there in the Garden of Gethsemane He prayed with those three.

Anybody can help us make some decisions. But there are other decisions that only those we love and appreciate most can help us make. Then, there are some decisions we have to make alone with God. So, Jesus went a little further, all alone, and there He prayed: "Nevertheless not my will, but thine, be done" (Luke 22:42).

The rock where it is believed that He knelt and prayed is still there. Many times I have knelt at that rock and I have prayed. Many more times in my imagination I have knelt at that rock as I have sought to make some decision according to God's will. It never is easy, and sometimes it is difficult. As Jesus made that decision He struggled so that even drops of blood popped out on His forehead.

We have decisions to make and we need to pray for God's will to be done.

However, that is not the end of the story about the Garden of Gethsemane. Some years ago when I was the minister of the Grace United Methodist Church in Atlanta, the church decided to replace the windows in the sanctuary. We wanted those twenty-eight windows to depict the life of Christ. We learned of a wonderful artist in England who had a small plant where he made stained-glass windows, and we invited him to visit with us and to help us plan. It was truly a thrilling experience to work with him in the planning of those windows which can be seen today in the sanctuary on Ponce de Leon Avenue. Whenever I have an opportunity, I like to go and look at those windows again.

We got along well in the planning of the windows until we came to the Gethsemane window. The artist showed me a drawing which he had made of Jesus kneeling by a rock. But I said to him that that was not the total picture. When he insisted that it was, I took the Bible and read a verse that most people do not seem to notice in reference to the Gethsemane story. That verse is: "And there appeared an angel unto him from heaven, strengthening him" (Luke 22:43). The artist redrew the painting to show Jesus kneeling at that rock, and the angel of God hovering over His shoulder.

The point is—God does not require us to make our decisions alone. He still sends angels to strengthen us when we need extra help. So here is the promise: "Whatsoever you ask in my name, if it is what you really want, and if it is in harmony with God's larger purposes and will, then God and you working together will bring it to pass."

With that assurance we can look toward the future with confidence instead of fear.

From my readings I have especially marked two paragraphs that I would like for us to think about at this moment. Marguerite Higgins, a war correspondent, received the much-coveted Pulitzer Prize for international reporting of the Korean struggle. In her articles she records many interesting and poignant experiences. One such is found in her account of the Fifth Company of marines, which originally numbered eighteen thousand men; they were engaged in combat with more than one hundred thousand Chinese Communists. That morning it was cold, forty-two degrees below zero. The weary soldiers, half-frozen, stood by their dirty trucks, eating from tin cans. A huge marine was eating cold beans with his trench knife, his clothes as stiff as a board; his face, covered with heavy beard, was crusted with mud. A correspondent asked him, "If I were God and could grant you anything you wished, what would you most like?" The man stood motionless for a moment, then he raised his head and replied, "Give me tomorrow."

The other paragraph I am remembering also comes from the annals of war. Over the portal of the allied cemetery in North Assam, where lie the bodies of many American soldiers who fought in India and Burma during the Second World War, are these words: "Tell Them That We Gave Our Todays For Their Tomorrows."

We can find great inspiration in those words. Look back over your life and think about the people who have given some of their todays for your tomorrows. Think of parents, relatives, neighbors, friends, schoolteachers, and many others who befriended you. This gives us inspiration to realize that as we are faithful today we are making someone's tomorrow. It may be our own tomorrow and very likely it will be somebody else's tomorrow too.

Tomorrow is a marvelous inspiration for living.

Fourteen

The Five Laws of Faith _____

We all know that it takes faith to keep going, but after a very disturbing experience in one's life—the death of a loved one, a serious illness, a business reversal—one has a tendency to be almost paralyzed and completely defeated. Certainly the loss of one's marriage is one of those traumatic, difficult times. Divorce can bring so many unhappy thoughts—shame, failure, defeat, lack of hope—even surrender.

Some years ago I wrote a book entitled *Prayer Changes Things* and in it I talked about the laws of faith. Now I would like to reaffirm those same laws. The Bible tells us, "Without faith it is impossible to please God . . ." (Hebrews 11:6). I might add, without faith it is impossible to please ourselves. So let's consider five laws of faith.

The First Law of Faith

Rabbi Louis Binstock told about a man who had all the financial resources he needed, community standing, and every reasonable hope for happiness. He appeared to have everything, yet he came to the rabbi to say that he had "nothing for which to live."

The man was desperate. When the rabbi said, "You are in the House of God. . . . Give yourself over to the grace of His peace," the man's eyes flashed with bitterness. "The same oldtime bunk. . . . Have faith in the Lord—and presto! all your troubles are over and life is beautiful forever afterwards." The man was not interested in that. He got up and reached for his hat.

The rabbi seized his arm and pulled him back. There was an "I-won't-find-help-here" look in the man's eyes, and the rabbi talked slowly: "You are going to help yourself. You have access to a great storehouse of dynamic power, but you have not been using it. That storehouse is faith."

The man's mouth curled with contempt: "If I possessed such a storehouse of faith, would I come to you? Sure, I need faith. But how do I get it? Where can I find it?" He was not the last man who has asked those questions about faith: Where can I find it? How do I get it?

In answer, the rabbi told him an old Chinese tale about a little fish who once overheard one fisherman say to another, "Have you ever stopped to think how essential water is to life? Without water our earth would dry up. Every living thing would die." The fish became panic-stricken. "I must find some water at once! If not, in a few days I will be dead!" And the fish went swimming away as fast as he could. But where could he find water? He had never heard of it before.

He asked the other fish in the lake, but they didn't know. He swam out into the large river, but no fish there could tell him where to find water. He kept swimming until he reached the deepest place in the ocean. There he found an old and wise fish. He gasped, "Where can I find water?" The old fish chuckled. "Water? Why you are in it right now. You were in it back home in your own lake. You have never been out of it since the day you were born." The little fish began the long swim back home saying. "I had water all the time, and I didn't know it."

So it is with faith. You don't find faith. You don't get faith. You simply use faith that you already have. When a baby is born, God gives it faith just the same as He gives it hands and feet. A child needs to learn to walk, but it is born with the capacity to walk. The teacher cannot give a child intelligence; the teacher teaches the child to use its intelligence. The child cannot be given music; the teacher teaches the child to express the music it possesses.

As energy cannot be created or destroyed, neither can faith be. But faith can lie unused within us. It can be covered up and not used.

We Bury Faith Under Fears

We were born "bundles of faith." Nothing is more trusting than a child; but instead of developing that faith, we usually concentrate on teaching the child fear. We make sure that the child learns that knives will cut, cats will scratch, dogs will bite, fire will burn, automobiles will run over him, water will drown him, disobedience will bring a whipping, and ugly words will result in a mouth-washing with soap.

Downtown one day I actually heard a mother say to her little boy, "If you don't hush crying, I'll let that mean policeman yonder put you in the dark jail!" What a wonderful way to smother a child's faith with unreasonable fear.

As we grow older we learn other fears. A schoolboy can fail an examination; a bigger boy can teach a little boy how much a lick of the fist can hurt; a teenager can be socially slighted. We can learn the meaning of privation; we experience the disappointments of love, the pain of a broken heart, the disillusionment of the treachery of a friend, the shock of business failure, the burden of a sense of guilt.

It's no wonder that many people who have so emphasized their fears have had their faith buried and forgotten. A scientific magazine sometime ago declared that all normal children possess qualities of genius. When you think of your own precious little one as a genius, you are entirely correct. The article claimed that mediocrity doesn't occur until later life. All children are geniuses, but hardly any adults. What happens? No one loses his mental power, but our power becomes buried.

Study closely the dealings of Christ with people and you will see that this was the basic principle by which He worked. He changed people by releasing them. There was Matthew who had let greed make him a slick traitor to his own people. Jesus did not condemn him; He held before Matthew the vision of the highest. Like a magnet drawing a piece of steel, the vision of his possibilities drew out Matthew's real self and made him Saint Matthew. Jesus used His power to make people believe in themselves, and that worked the miracle of change.

There is a heartwarming play called *Seventh Heaven*. It opens with the return of Chicot, the battle-blinded French soldier. He has come back to his sweetheart, who had starved and suffered in a dismal attic room, but she had never faltered in the conviction that her Chicot would return. In her joy of being with him again, she cries that she now can live in her "seventh heaven." He replies, "If you believe it, it's so—if you believe it, it's so."

Faith is not believing something that isn't so. Jesus taught that if we believe something, it will become so. He said, "What things soever ye desire, when ye pray, believe that ye receive them, and ye shall have them" (Mark 11:24).

We All Live by Faith

How can I get faith? Where can I find it? You don't get faith—you already have it. The only place you can find it is within yourself. And the only way you can find it is to look for your faith instead of your fears and your failures.

People die, businesses fail, automobiles are wrecked, jobs are lost, homes are broken up, friends are betrayed, lives are ruined. When you fill your mind with that sort of thing, no wonder you lose sight of your faith and think you have lost it. But just for one day, keep a list of the times you express faith. You will be surprised.

I step out of bed in the morning onto the floor. I believe the floor will hold me up. I take a drink of water. The water comes from a muddy river contaminated with filth. In many places in the world a person would not dare drink water until it was boiled. But I drink the water believing it has been purified. I eat scrambled eggs for breakfast. My wife could have put arsenic in the eggs, but I have faith that she didn't.

I stop at the filling station for ten gallons of gasoline. I don't have a can to measure the gas—I have faith that I'll get what I pay for. I stop at the mailbox to mail a payment on my life insurance. I am depending on that insurance to mean a lot to my wife and children if I should die, to help me if I should get sick, to be a friend to me if I should be unable to work when I am old. That insurance means a lot to me, yet I mail the payments to an office I have never seen, to be handled by people I will never know. I have faith that they will do what they say. Space doesn't permit the naming of the many times I use faith in one day.

Along with sixty-eight other people, I got on an airplane one day. As we were waiting for the plane to take off, I got to figuring how much sixty-eight people weighed. Allowing 150 pounds per person, the total was more than 10,000 pounds. Their baggage added another 2,000 pounds. Then I got to figuring the weight of the plane. It must have been as much as 50,000 pounds—maybe twice that much. Then I began thinking—in a few moments we would be going down that runway at 150 miles per hour. Beyond the end of the runway I could see tall trees and big rocks on the ground. If we went into those trees and rocks we would all be killed. But I looked at the big motors on the plane and I believed they had the power to lift that big plane above the trees. Looking at only the weight, I was fearful. Looking at the motors, I had faith.

So it is in life. We automatically use faith in a thousand different ways; but sometimes when we come to a place when we must consciously use faith, we shrink back. Instead of thinking of your loads to lift, think of your own abilities, the support of other people, and especially the help of God. And as you think of your power instead of your problems, you will find that faith comes easily and naturally. And you will not then be afraid of failure.

You already have faith—that is the first law of faith.

Two More Laws of Faith

Every person has faith. Also, every person has fears. In life the difference is whether you start with your faith or with your fears. Some people think first of the difficulties when facing an undertaking; other people think of the possibilities.

There was a lady who had a stroke of paralysis which left her left leg severely crippled. She had great difficulty in learning to walk again. In fact, she surrendered to a rolling chair. Her doctor was a very wise man and he refused to let her stay in that chair. One day he told her to stand up; then he told her to walk. Slowly she put forward that crippled left leg, but she sank back in the chair unable to complete the step.

However, the doctor told her to stand up again. Then he told her to take the first step with her right leg, the one that was not paralyzed. She did that and she found that she could walk. The wise doctor then told her to remember that she could walk if she would always put her best foot forward. This is one of the essentials of faith. Start with your faith, and your paralyzing fears will not be able to hold you back.

One of my closest minister-friends is an example of this principle. When he was six years old, his older brother accidentally shot him. The bullet went through his right hand and his left arm. Several of his fingers were shot away and his left elbow was forever ruined. But that accident did not hurt his spirit. In fact, his crippled hand and arm caused him to develop his faith more completely.

He got through high school but then had no money for college. So he got an old typewriter, learned to type, and paid his expenses through college by working as a part-time secretary. He wanted a Ph. D. degree, so he went to Yale. For his doctor's dissertation, he chose a study of ninth-century manuscripts written in Vulgate Latin. He didn't know Vulgate Latin but he learned it. Also, in order to complete his research, he had to learn six other languages: Greek, Hebrew, German, French, Aramaic, and Syriac. To pay his expenses my friend worked in the cafeteria and at night he read proof in a newspaper office from 11 o'clock until 4 o'clock in the morning. He got his Ph. D. degree and also made an important contribution to biblical knowledge.

I have conducted two revivals in his church and stayed in his home during those weeks. We would talk until late at night and he greatly inspired me by his great courage and optimism. I said to him one night, "You might have held up your crippled hand and your undeveloped arm and given up in defeat."

He replied, "We all have limitations of some kind and we all have abilities. I thought about what I could do and never worried about anything else." He then said, "Our limitations can be either stepping stones or stopping places."

Start With Your Powers—
Not Your Problems

Whenever I get discouraged, there is no chapter in the Bible which lifts me up and gets me going again better than the fourth chapter of Philippians. I think of St. Paul, who wrote those words. He was a man severely handicapped in body. After he became a man, he never had a home of his own or a loved one who belonged to him.

I think of how he was beaten with sticks and rocks, thrown into jails, and how his frail body must have shivered from the cold. Many times he was hungry. He had a task of preaching Christ to the world, yet against him was the most powerful and ruthless government the world had ever known. In that fourth chapter I think we find revealed the secrets of his great power and unconquerable will.

He writes, "Rejoice in the Lord always: and again I say, Rejoice" (v.4). That is, no matter what happens, don't get down in the mouth. Think of God instead of your troubles and express your joy. One of the strongest allies of faith is a smile on our faces.

Also he writes, ". . . whatsoever things are true, . . . honest, . . . just, . . . pure, . . . lovely, . . . of good report . . . think on these things" (v.8). We all have infirmities of some kind. There is something that hurts and holds you back, but instead of concentrating on your troubles, lift your mind to things that will lift you.

In that same chapter Paul says, "I have learned, in whatsoever state I am, therewith to be content" (v.11). Instead of rebelling against the circumstances of his life, he had learned that in any situation there are opportunities.

Then he gives the secret of his amazing strength, the reason he is never defeated. He declares, "I can do all things through Christ, which strengtheneth me" (v.13). It makes a tremendous difference when you are not totally dependent on yourself.

Also St. Paul gives the reason for his quiet confidence: ". . . my God shall supply all your need . . ." (v.19). With that assurance, one finds it easy to approach life with faith instead of fear. Every person has limitations and every person has assets. The difference in people lies in whether they start with their problems or with their powers, whether they first step forward with faith or with fear.

The other night I was reading one of Jack London's books. I thought about him. He was nineteen years old before he ever got a chance to go to high school. He died when he was forty years old. Yet he published fifty-one thrilling books.

Lord Byron and Sir Walter Scott each had a clubfoot and were forced to limp their ways through life. John Milton and Homer, two of the greatest writers of all time, were totally blind. When F. W. Woolworth got his first job in a store, his employers would not let him wait on the customers because they said he was too stupid. But men like these will live forever because they emphasized their assets instead of their weaknesses.

Hold On to Your Faith

Someone has pointed out that we live in two worlds—the world that is and the world we want it to be. Faith takes hold of the world that is, and makes it what we want it to be. Faith takes the possible and makes it real. It was the great William James who said, "As the essence of courage is to stake one's life on a possibility, so the essence of faith is to believe that the possibility exists." And believing that a better tomorrow is possible, we do have the courage to give our best to the creating of that tomorrow.

The first three laws of faith are these: (1) know that you have faith; (2) start with your faith instead of your fears; (3) no matter what happens, hold on to your faith.

People in Vienna delight in swimming in the Danube River. One of their favorite sports is going up to one of the higher levels of the great river and swimming down toward the center of the city. But every year a few of the swimmers are caught in the whirlpools and drowned.

An expert swimmer says that all such drownings could easily be avoided. He says that water, if given a chance, will always push human beings toward the surface. But one must trust the water. When caught in a whirlpool, many swimmers become panic-stricken and are drowned. However, all one has to do is hold his breath for a few moments and the water will thrust him clear and he can easily swim to safety.

So it is in the stream of life. We have the faith to start off on some high adventure. We are happy in our hopes and confidently we move forward. Then we become caught in some whirlpool of life, and instead of making progress, are violently thrown around. Our strokes lose their natural rhythm. We become panic-stricken; we press harder or surrender to failure. But if we hold on to our faith it will never fail us.

One of the grandest men of our time, or of any time, is Winston Churchill. But back in 1915 he was demoted from an important position and branded as a failure. For twenty-five years he was lost in political obscurity. But though he was lost from public eye, he never lost his faith. In 1940 the stream of life pushed him to the surface again and he was ready to write one of England's most glorious chapters.

In this connection we quickly think of Columbus. He had faith in a great idea. But his friends deserted him, his wife died, and he was even forced to beg for bread. He waited and worked for seven long years before he got enough help to begin his journey across the sea.

For sixty-seven days he sailed. Storms ravaged his ships, his men threatened mutiny; but Columbus stayed with his faith. It was as Joaquin Miller wrote:

> *What shall we do when hope is gone?*
> *Sail on! Sail on! Sail on! and on!*

And Columbus discovered a new world.

Don't give up your faith. There is a new world ahead for you, too.

Another and Another of Faith's Laws

Now, I want to set down one of the supreme principles of faith. It is: Don't be afraid to trust your heart. I got it from a young couple who had come to talk with me about their plans for marriage. It seemed that it would be very difficult for this marriage to succeed and I discussed with them some of the obstacles in their path to happiness together.

There were considerable differences in their backgrounds, both financially and socially. They were of different religious faiths, and I pointed out how each could be hurt in the years to come. There were some other problems. I really hoped they would decide to take more time and possibly reconsider.

Finally the girl spoke up. I had much admiration for her because of the circumstances under which I had come to know her. Once I had been on an airplane which ran into a rather heavy storm. In the turbulent air, the plane was pushed around considerably. Some of the passengers got sick and the rest of us got mighty scared. This girl was the stewardess on that plane and she moved among the passengers with a calmness and courage that was wonderful to see. Now, feeling the threat of some stormy weather which might lie ahead in her flight into matrimony, she was no less calm and her answer was wonderful. She said, "We love each other and we are not afraid to trust our hearts."

Recently I was preaching in another city, and after the service this couple came up to speak to me. I had not seen them since their marriage and I had wondered how it was with them. She said, "You need never worry about us. We have risen above the storms and we have clear sailing."

It was Pascal who said, "The heart has reasons which reason does not know." Not only in marriage, but in most of life's high ventures, in order to have faith you must learn to trust your heart. Faith is never unreasonable, yet there are times when feeling is stronger than reason and we must sometimes trust those deep inner impulses.

Dr. Norman Peale tells of one morning when he was in a Sunday School class. Along with the other boys, he was listening to the teacher tell about the courage and faith of Christ as He turned His face toward Jerusalem. It meant meeting His enemies head-on. It meant a cross. But He did not hesitate. The teacher said, "I wonder if any boy in this class is willing to follow Him."

Twelve-year-old Norman Peale felt something happen in his heart in that moment, something that reason could never explain. From then on that feeling in his heart became the guiding force in his life. It led him into the ministry—and what a glorious ministry his has been! But the Dr. Peale the world knows today would never have been if he had been afraid to trust his heart.

One of the most moving scenes in the life of our Lord occurred one morning after breakfast. The trials and the cross were now behind Him, and He was soon to go back to the Father's house. But what about the future of His work on earth? He had come to build a church, to establish a Kingdom, to bring all mankind into brotherhood, peace, and righteousness.

Was it all an impossible dream? Would His coming result in failure and defeat? It depended, I think, on one man—Simon Peter. Simon did not have the education, culture, and mental ability of some of the other disciples, but he was a natural leader of men. The direction Simon took would be the direction they would all take.

It was now only a few days before the Lord's ascension. During breakfast that morning, He must have been thinking of how

Simon had denied Him during the trials; how, when courage was
called for, Simon had played the part of the coward. After breakfast Jesus slipped over by Simon's side. He might have embar-
rassed His disciple before the others, but He did not even
mention his shameful failure. Instead He said, "Simon, . . . lovest
thou me . . .?" (John 21:15). He did not argue with Simon; He
simply wanted to know what was in his heart. And Jesus was not
afraid to trust a man's heart.

In truth, Jesus always knew that if He could capture a man's
heart He would have the man; so His method of winning people
was through the heart. We recall how a rich young ruler came to
Him, and the Bible says, "Jesus beholding him loved him . . ."
(Mark 10:21). If the young man had returned that love, his life
would have been forever different. Maybe he did love Jesus, but
was afraid to trust his heart.

Faith is never blind. Faith is never unreasonable. But there are
times when the only guide we have to our rendezvous with des-
tiny is the faith in our hearts.

Certainly Jesus was not afraid to trust His heart. His method
of winning men is through loving men. As little children we learn
to sing:

> Jesus loves me, this I know,
> For the Bible tells me so.

And in old age we sing:

> Jesus, Lover of my soul,
> Let me to Thy bosom fly.

You do not doubt His love for you, yet it often seems unreasonable. We are such a mixture of good and bad that we are
ashamed of ourselves. An old British soldier wrote these words:

> My padre, he says I'm a sinner,
> John Bull, he says I'm a saint,
> But they are both of them bound to be liars,
> For I'm neither of them—I ain't.

> *For I'm a man, and a man is a mixture*
> *Right down from his very birth.*
> *Part of him comes from heaven*
> *And part of him comes from earth.*

Jesus knows that, but He still loves us; and because He trusts His heart, He never loses faith in us. We too must learn to trust our hearts.

Maintain a Spirit of Humility

If one wishes to possess and keep a calm, confident faith as he goes through life, it is absolutely essential for one to maintain a spirit of humility. Faith and humility go together, and without one the other quickly dies.

Out of Catholic tradition comes this wonderful story. There was a rumor that a girl in a convent was performing almost unbelievable miracles. The Pope sent St. Philip of Neri to investigate. After a long journey, he finally reached the convent and asked to see the girl. As she entered the room, he pulled off his muddy boots and asked her to clean them. Haughtily she drew up her shoulders and scornfully turned away. St. Philip left and when he got back to the Pope, he said, "His Holiness must give no credence to the rumors. Where there is no humility, there can be no miracles."

Maybe St. Philip was thinking of the time when the Lord of lords poured water in a basin, got on His knees, and began to wash the disciples' feet. And how He spoke to them that night of the temptations to come within the next days. And how Simon Peter loudly boasted that though everybody else might deny the Lord, He could depend on Simon to hold steady and firm. And how after that supper they went out into the garden and Jesus got on His knees to pray to God, but those disciples felt no need of prayer; they were sufficient unto themselves. Certainly it is true—where there is no humility, there are no miracles.

There is a story of a young college girl who visited the home of Beethoven. She asked permission to play on the great master's piano. She played a few bars and then said to the guard, "I suppose all the great artists have played this piano during their visits here?" He replied, "No, Paderewski was here two years ago and someone asked him to play. But he declined, saying he was not worthy to touch that piano." All great people are humble. That is why they are great.

The pattern is set forth in 2 Chronicles 7:14: "If my people, which are called by my name, shall humble themselves, and pray, and seek my face, and turn from their wicked ways. . . ." Notice, we are never taught in the Bible to ask for humility; we are to humble ourselves. Every Sunday night while I was pastor I invited people to come and kneel at the altar. Occasionally I was asked if one cannot pray as well sitting in the pews. My answer was, "I can't." I think there is much value in the act of kneeling. In itself, it is a humbling experience.

When one is humble, he does not feel self-sufficient. Then it is easier to pray, to seek God, and turn away from wrong. The remainder of that verse tells us what God will do after our humility, prayer, true seeking of Him, and forsaking of wrong: ". . . then will I hear from heaven, and will forgive their sin, and will heal their land"; that is, God will hear, forgive, and bring peace and prosperity. When we meet the conditions and the promise of God is fulfilled, we are afraid of nothing and we face the future with serene confidence.

Fifteen

Today—
Today—
Today

In previous pages we have been talking about yesterday and tomorrow. It is very important to talk about both of those. Now we need to get down to today—this very day.

The psalmist put it in a thrilling and wonderful way: "This is the day which the Lord has made; we will rejoice and be glad in it" (Psalms 118:24). There comes a time when we need to think about what we are going to do today. We can't go back and undo yesterday. We can dream about tomorrow, but we can't live it. The only day we can live is this day.

121

It was the great surgeon Doctor William Osler who said, "The load of tomorrow, added to that of yesterday, carried today, makes the strongest falter. We must learn to shut off the future as tightly as the past."

I like the lines which were written by Pearl Yeadon McGinnis. I do not know their source, but she wrote:

> *I have no YESTERDAYS,*
> *Time took them away;*
> *Tomorrow may not be—*
> *But I have TODAY.*

I think no one ever put it better than Dale Carnegie when he said, "One of the most tragic things I know about human nature is that all of us tend to put off living. We are all thinking of some magical rose garden over the horizon—instead of enjoying the roses that are blooming outside our windows today."

Many years ago, I found the following poem in a magazine. I memorized it and have quoted it literally hundreds of times. It has been one of the most inspirational poems of my life.

> *If you can't be a pine on the top of the hill,*
> *Be a scrub in the valley—but be*
> *The best little scrub by the side of the rill;*
> *Be a bush if you can't be a tree.*
>
> *If you can't be a bush be a bit of the grass,*
> *And some highway happier make;*
> *If you can't be a muskie then just be a bass—*
> *But be the liveliest bass in the lake!*
>
> *We can't all be captains, we've got to be crew,*
> *There's something for all of us here,*
> *There's big work to do, and there's lesser to do,*
> *And the task you must do is the near.*
>
> *If you can't be a highway then just be a trail,*
> *If you can't be a sun be a star;*
> *It isn't by size that you win or you fail—*
> *Be the best of whatever you are!*

That poem has strong inspiration for me. I have realized through the years that there are many talents I do not have. One of the things people have teased me about is my singing. Sometimes when I am in the pulpit I get carried away with the singing and sing out with all my gusto, not realizing that I am standing right in front of the microphone. Many people who have heard me over television or radio have told me that I ought not to sing. Really and truly I wish I could sing. I get great inspiration out of music and I think I have felt a little disappointment that I could not musically perform. But then one day one of the bishops in our church heard someone teasing me about my singing. The bishop said to me, "Charles, do not worry about not being able to sing. In all of my career I have never had a church say to me that they wanted a certain preacher because he could sing so well." That made me feel better. God has given me more opportunities than I dreamed I would ever have. I do not have to be a singer. The important thing is, "Be the best of whatever you are!"

That poem has meant so much to me and recently I got a genuine thrill when I learned who wrote it. It was written by Douglas Malloch, who was born in 1877 and died in 1938. Some of his poems may have been published in books but I have not been able to locate them. However, just recently I discovered another poem Mr. Malloch wrote. It too is wonderful and worthy of consideration.

"It's Fine Today"

Sure, this world is full of trouble—
I ain't said it ain't.
Lord, I've had enough and double
Reason for complaint;
Rain and storm have come to fret me,
Skies are often gray;
Thorns and brambles have beset me
On the road—but say,
Ain't it fine today?

What's the use of always weepin'
Making trouble last?
What's the use of always keepin'
Thinking of the past?
Each must have his tribulation—
Water with his wine;
Life, it ain't no celebration,
Trouble?—I've had mine—
But today is fine!

It's today that I am livin',
Not a month ago.
Having; losing; taking; givin';
Time wills it so.
Yesterday a cloud of sorrow
Fell across the way;
It may rain again tomorrow,
It may rain—but say,
Ain't it fine today?

I love Douglas Malloch for writing those two poems. The first one I've used for many, many years and now I have memorized the second one too. It will be with me the remainder of my life. When I am tempted to worry about either the past or the future, I am going to keep saying over and over to myself—"Ain't it fine today?"

In the Bible we are warned, "Boast not thyself of tomorrow; for thou knowest not what a day may bring forth" (Proverbs 27:1). That verse does not mean that we are not to plan and dream and think about the future. Life demands that we plan for tomorrow. Go back in history and think about all the contributions to our society made by people who planned ahead. Columbus dreamed of a new world and sailed forth across the Atlantic. Because he dreamed of what he might find tomorrow, we now have America. I have been saying in these pages that we should all plan greater things and a better, nobler life for tomorrow. However, the Bible warns us that you cannot boast about the things that you are going to do tomorrow. In the first place, you do not even know that you will be here tomorrow; and in the second place, even if you are here, you are not sure you are going to accomplish all of those dreams.

It can be very inspiring to think about tomorrow, but on the other hand it can also be very damaging and dangerous. We can excuse our lack of effort today by saying we are going to make up for it tomorrow. That is the road that leads to failure and disappointment.

An old legend has it that once Satan gathered all of his assistants around him and in a loud voice asked each one what he would do to destroy people on the earth. Each demon volunteered and set forth a strategy.

One said, "I will persuade them there is no heaven."

Satan replied, "No, that would not succeed because you could never convince mankind there is no heaven."

A second assistant of Satan said, "I will persuade people that there is no hell."

Satan answered, "That will not do because you could never persuade all of the people there is no hell."

One by one his assistants suggested what he would do to destroy the faith of humanity and one by one they were rejected.

Finally, the last one spoke up and said, "I will go."

"And what will you tell the people on the earth that will destroy them?" asked Satan.

"I will tell them," answered the last assistant, "that there is a heaven and there is a hell, but there is no need to think about either one of them today."

Satan replied, "You are the one I'm going to send because you are the one who will succeed."

We know this is just a legend, the figment of somebody's imagination, but we also know that the way to destroy a life is to simply say *I know it is something I should do or should not do, but I do not have to deal with it today.*

> *He was going to be all that a mortal should be*
> *To-morrow.*
> *No one should be kinder or braver than he*
> *To-morrow.*

A friend who was troubled and weary he knew,
Who'd be glad of a lift and who needed it, too;
On him he would call and see what he could do
To-morrow.

Each morning he stacked up letters he'd write
To-morrow.
And thought of the folks he would fill with delight
To-morrow.
It was too bad, indeed, he was busy to-day,
And hadn't a minute to stop on his way;
Nor time he would to give others, he'd say,
To-morrow.

The greatest of workers this man would have been
To-morrow.
The world would have known him, had he ever seen
To-morrow.
But the fact is he died and he faded from view,
And all that he left here when living was through
Was a mountain of things he intended to do
To-morrow.

Edgar A. Guest

As I have said earlier, a traumatic experience in life—such as a divorce—tends to almost paralyze the individual. You don't feel you can do anything. You give your thinking to yesterday and to tomorrow.

Let us reaffirm the fact that today really is the day that God has made, and let us rejoice that we have the opportunity to live this day. And by the grace of God, let's do it.

Some there are that torment themselves afresh with the memory of what is past; others, again, afflict themselves with the apprehension of evils to come; and very ridiculous boast—for the one does not now concern us, and the other not yet. . . .

One should count each day a separate life.

Each one can carry his burden, however hard, until nightfall. Anyone can do his work, however hard, for one day. Anyone can live sweetly, patiently, lovingly, purely, till the sun goes down. This is all that life really means.

Robert Louis Stevenson